ANNIE
OAKLEY

Other titles in *Historical American Biographies*

Annie Oakley
Legendary Sharpshooter
ISBN 0-7660-1012-0

John Wesley Powell
Explorer of the Grand Canyon
ISBN 0-89490-783-2

Benjamin Franklin
Founding Father and Inventor
ISBN 0-89490-784-0

Lewis and Clark
Explorers of the Northwest
ISBN 0-7660-1016-3

Buffalo Bill Cody
Western Legend
ISBN 0-7660-1015-5

Martha Washington
First Lady
ISBN 0-7660-1017-1

Clara Barton
Civil War Nurse
ISBN 0-89490-778-6

Paul Revere
Rider for the Revolution
ISBN 0-89490-779-4

Jeb Stuart
Confederate Cavalry General
ISBN 0-7660-1013-9

Robert E. Lee
Southern Hero of the Civil War
ISBN 0-89490-782-4

Jefferson Davis
President of the Confederacy
ISBN 0-7660-1064-3

Stonewall Jackson
Confederate General
ISBN 0-89490-781-6

Jesse James
Legendary Outlaw
ISBN 0-7660-1055-4

Susan B. Anthony
Voice for Women's Voting Rights
ISBN 0-89490-780-8

Thomas Alva Edison
Inventor
ISBN 0-7660-1014-7

Historical American Biographies

ANNIE OAKLEY

Legendary Sharpshooter

Jean Flynn

Enslow Publishers, Inc.

44 Fadem Road	PO Box 38
Box 699	Aldershot
Springfield, NJ 07081	Hants GU12 6BP
USA	UK

For Colin Don'l Flynn Bass

Library of Congress Cataloging-in-Publication Data

Flynn, Jean, 1934–
    Annie Oakley : legendary sharpshooter / Jean Flynn.
       p. cm. — (Historical American biographies)
    Includes bibliographical references and index.
    Summary: Recounts the life of the markswoman and performer who achieved fame with Buffalo Bill Cody's Wild West Show.
    ISBN 0-7660-1012-0
    1. Oakley, Annie, 1860–1926—Juvenile literature. 2. Shooters of firearms—United States—Biography—Juvenile literature. 3. Women entertainers—United States—Biography—Juvenile literature. 4. Frontier and pioneer life—West (U.S.)—Juvenile literature. [1. Oakley, Annie, 1860–1926. 2. Sharpshooters. 3. Women entertainers. 4. Entertainers. 5. Women—Biography.] I. Title. II. Series.
GV1157.03F59 1998
799.3'092
[B]—DC21
                                          97-25394
                                               CIP
                                             AC

Illustration Credits: The Darke County Historical Society, Inc., Greenville, Ohio, pp. 12, 14, 22, 28, 31, 34, 39, 45, 46, 53, 69, 73, 78, 90, 96, 99, 103, 104, 109, 113; Reproduced from the *Dictionary of American Portraits*, published by Dover Publications, Inc., in 1967, pp. 43, 55; Enslow Publishers, Inc., p. 83.

Cover Illustrations: © Corel Corporation (background); Reproduced from the *Dictionary of American Portraits*, published by Dover Publications, Inc., in 1967 (inset).

Contents

1

THE CONTEST

Fifteen-year-old Annie Moses could shoot the head off a quail at thirty yards, but she could not read. In 1875, it was not unusual for women to be unable to read. Yet it was unusual for a young woman from a Quaker family to be a crack shot with a rifle. Annie had more practice shooting than she did reading. By the time she was fifteen, she already had a reputation as a sharpshooter. She had been known as the best shot in Darke County, Ohio, for years. Before the end of her life, she would become famous as one of the best sharpshooters in the world.

She first started hunting for her family's food. Then, she earned money by selling the wild game her family could not use to Charles Katzenberger of Greenville. When she brought in more than he could use, he sold the surplus to hotels in Cincinnati, Ohio. The hotel keepers preferred to buy Annie's game because the quails, rabbits, squirrels, and pheasants were shot through the head. Their guests never complained of buckshot in their meat. In three years, Annie saved enough money to pay off the mortgage on her mother and stepfather's house.[1]

Susan Shaw, Annie's mother, had often depended on Annie for meat to feed her large family. However, as a Quaker, Mrs. Shaw disapproved of firearms. As Annie approached the age when many young women got married, Mrs. Shaw wanted her to experience something besides hunting. Annie knew nothing about the world outside Darke County.

Mrs. Shaw took Annie to visit Lydia Stein, Annie's older sister, in Fairmount, near Cincinnati, Ohio. Just eighty miles from Annie's birthplace, Cincinnati was a place of wonder for Annie. From the top of steep streets in Fairmount, Annie could see the great city two miles away. It was like another world. She was used to the quiet of the fields and woods. She "saw a real city then for the first time."[2]

A Born Hunter

Annie Oakley described her talent as a sharpshooter as something she had since birth. She said:

> I believe I was born with a fondness for shooting. My earliest recollections are of the times I would smuggle my brother's musket away to the woods and shoot game.[3]

Seeing New Sights

It was on a steep hill in Fairmount that Annie first saw a gun club. One day, she saw a sign that read, "Schuetzenbuckel." Annie asked her sister what it meant. Lydia explained that it was a German word that means "Shooter's Hill." Only men were allowed in the gun club, where they practiced target shooting and held exhibitions of their skills. It was the first time Annie heard about using guns for pleasure shooting. She thought they were used only for necessities, such as hunting and protection from Indian attacks.[4] When she became a champion sharpshooter, Annie opened the doors of gun clubs to women in the United States and Europe.

Lydia's husband, Joe Stein, showed Annie Cincinnati's nightlife. She saw everything from the horrors in a wax museum to the stuffed wild animals in the basement of Robinson's Opera House.[5]

One night, as she wandered with Joe from sight to sight, Annie recognized the sound of gunshots.

They were near Charlie Stuttelberg's shooting gallery. Shooting galleries were as new to Annie as gun clubs were. She was interested in seeing what they were like. Unlike the gun club, which was closed to females, the shooting gallery was open to anyone.

Annie saw targets lined up on a metal track against a back wall. Gaslights flickered over a row of metal ducks, a row of big-eared rabbits, and a red bull's-eye surrounded by black circles. They looked like easy targets to Annie. Guns lay idle on the countertop separating the shooter from the target range. Stein decided they should try their luck. He shot six times and hit two ducks. Then he gave the gun to Annie.

Charlie Stuttelberg sat on a box in a corner behind the counter. He looked at Annie over the top of the newspaper he was reading. "No charge if you ring the bell five times," he said as he grinned.[6] Annie put the gun to her shoulder and aimed at the targets.

There was no lapse of time between the ringing of the bells. Stuttelberg slowly folded his newspaper. His eyes narrowed as he looked at the slim, young girl. "The next round is free," he said, all trace of his smile gone.[7]

Annie smiled and aimed. Six shots fired. Six hits. Stuttelberg's eyes bulged and his mouth dropped open. Annie had hit the bull's-eye and five ducks in a row. He was impressed and insisted she talk to Jack Frost, operator of a hotel, about entering a shooting match.[8]

Frost had known about Annie for some time, but he had never met her. For years, he had bought Annie's game for his hotel. He already knew how good a shot she was.

A Shooting Match

Frost suggested a match between Annie and Frank Butler, a professional sharpshooter who was appearing at a local theater. When Butler questioned Frost about his opponent, Frost said she was, "Just an unknown, who thinks [she] can shoot."[9]

Butler was never opposed to making extra money. The winner's prize was fifty dollars, a lot of money in 1875. Without knowing who his opponent was, Butler agreed to the match. He thought he would be matched against some "country sucker" who did not have a chance to win.[10] He bragged that he could outshoot "anything living, save Carver or Bogardus," two outstanding marksmen of the day.[11]

As confident as he was, Butler never bet on his own ability. The prize money was enough. The excitement and competition was what he liked. He

Annie Oakley entered her first sharpshooting competition at the age of fifteen.

later said, "You may bet, however, that I almost dropped dead when a slim little girl in short dresses stepped out to the mark with me."[12]

Annie had never been on a shooting range or shot at targets released from a mechanical trap. She was used to wild game in the open fields and trees. But if Annie was nervous, she did not show it.[13]

Annie and Butler stood on each side of the referee as he tossed a coin in the air. Butler won the toss. He took his position for the first shot. There were two traps to release the clay targets, called pigeons. Their guns were held below the elbow. Only one barrel was to be used. Nothing was said except "Pull!" to release a "pigeon" and "Dead!" if a target was hit.[14] Annie and Butler took turns shooting.

The quietness of the crowd magnified the loud, echoing sound of the guns. Annie and Butler had twenty-four shots and twenty-four hits each. Annie had matched Butler shot for shot. It was Butler's turn again.

"Pull!" Butler yelled. The target shot out of the trap, fluttered sideways, and then bobbed up and down in the air. Bang! The tense crowd groaned. Frank Butler had missed!

Annie had to hit the last pigeon to win. Her knees were shaking. She saw her mother's and sister's faces and knew she could do it. Young Annie blocked out everything around her. Her only focus

When Annie Moses won a contest with Frank Butler, she did not know that she would one day wear medals for sharpshooting from many countries.

was hitting the target. The crowd once again became silent. Annie lined the gun up, then dropped it quickly below the elbow.[15]

"Pull!" she yelled.

"Bang!" rang out instantly through the stillness of the air as Annie shot at the target.

"Dead!" shouted the referee.

The crowd went wild.

Annie had hit her twenty-fifth target. She had won the contest!

Annie turned to her opponent and smiled. Frank Butler was stunned, but he did not feel humiliated about his loss. He had fallen in love.[16]

2

A SHORT CHILDHOOD

Phoebe Ann Moses was born on August 13, 1860, in Darke County, Ohio. She was the fifth daughter of Jacob and Susan Moses. Their first three daughters—Mary Jane, Lydia, and Elizabeth—were born in Blair County, Pennsylvania, where Jacob Moses owned a small inn near the Pennsylvania Canal at Hollidaysburg. He was not a wealthy man, but his family had all the necessities of life. That changed in 1855 when a careless guest knocked over an oil lamp and the inn burned to the ground.

Jacob Moses was a poor man when he arrived in Ohio, with a growing family and an old Kentucky rifle. Yet he was determined and strong and ready to make a new start. He chose a plot of land just outside Woodland, a tiny village eighteen miles from Greenville, to build a new home.

Moses built a one-room log cabin from trees on his free land. The floor was hard-packed clay. The fireplace served both as a place to cook and a source of heat. Furniture was made from cut, split, and shaved logs. Mattresses were made of homespun ticking stuffed with straw.

A Growing Family

There was hardly space to move as the family grew in number. Sarah Ellen was born in 1857 and Catherine, who died in infancy, was born in 1859. Born in 1860, Phoebe Ann, the sixth daughter, was soon nicknamed Annie.[1] It was not until their only son, John, was born in 1862 that the Moseses added another room to the house. Two more children were born in the log cabin—a daughter Hulda in 1864, and an unnamed son, who died soon after birth in 1865.

Like all settlers, the Moseses had to use all of their energy and intelligence to survive. They made use of everything possible from the land and animals. Annie's mother canned and dried as many fresh fruits and vegetables as she could and then packed the rest in straw. Nut and berry picking were activities for the children. Nuts were plentiful and wild berries were a welcome change of diet. Game was plentiful in the dense forest surrounding the Woodland settlement. Annie's father shot or trapped game. The family used the meat and furs.

Every year, Annie's father butchered a steer or cow that he had raised for food, and smoked the meat with hickory chips to keep it from spoiling. Then, he tanned its hide for shoes for the family. "The measurements were taken and the shoes made from daddy down," Annie explained.[2] As the family's provider, Mr. Moses made sturdy shoes for himself first, then for Mrs. Moses and the children, according to age and outdoor chores.

Grain and vegetables were raised on the small farm, but the land could not produce enough food or income to support such a large family. Even though Jacob Moses took a job carrying the mail, the family struggled to survive.

Annie was a small child, strong despite her size, with thick dark hair. People often noticed her eyes, which were blue-gray, large, and bright with a direct gaze. She was an admitted tomboy who took no interest in her sisters' rag dolls. She liked working and hunting with her father and her brother John. When she was not with them, she spent hours wandering through the woods, listening to the birds, and tracking rabbits.

Annie's Carefree Life Changes

In the fall of 1865, when Annie was only five years old, her father left on a cold gray morning to take the grain to the gristmill to be ground into flour. It looked like it might snow, but he needed to make the trip before the long winter set in. High drifts of snow would cut off the family from the mill and general store.

Annie's father took the grain to the mill and went to the store to buy supplies for the snowbound months ahead. By the time he started for home, it had begun to snow and the wind was blowing hard. Before long, he was caught in a blizzard, but he managed to get to his log house through deep drifts of snow and freezing wind.

It was past midnight when he returned. "Mother threw the door wide open into the face of the howling wind," Annie recalled.[3] Annie's father sat upright in the buckboard seat of the wagon. He had tied the ends of the reins together and hung them around his neck. His legs were frozen stiff like logs, and his fingers were curled tightly shut. How he had managed to stay on the wagon seat was a miracle. He had not guided the horses. They had found their own way home through the blinding snow. "We all carried him in someway, leaving the wagon right where it was until it was dug out of the snow two days later," Annie remembered.[4] The doctor came, but there was little he could do.[5]

At age five, Annie's carefree childhood ended with Jacob Moses's death in the spring of 1866. The next year, another tragedy struck. Annie's oldest sister, Mary Jane, died of overexposure to wet, cold weather and tuberculosis, a disease of the lungs. Mrs. Moses sacrificed the farm as well as the pet cow, Pink, to pay medical and funeral bills.

The dwindling family moved to a smaller farm that Mrs. Moses rented from a sympathetic neighbor. Annie's mother and the children did the housework, prepared food, made clothing, tended the animals, and farmed the land. "But every night," Annie remembered, "no matter how tired we all were, Mother washed our hands and feet, brushed and plaited our hair into pigtails, took little John and Baby Huldie onto her lap, and sang hymns with us and prayed God to watch over us."[6]

Meat for the Family

Annie was an independent little girl who already knew the ways of the forest and its creatures. Her father had taught her to make traps out of cornstalks. Using the large end of the cornstalk, she made a log house tied together with string, leaving a small opening near the bottom. After spreading grain in a narrow trench that slanted upward into the opening in the "house," she covered it with brush. There was just enough room for a small animal or bird to slip into the trap. After it had eaten, it could not get out again. By the time she was seven, Annie was trapping quails, squirrels, and pheasants for the family table. She kept several traps set and checked them every day. There was always meat to eat. Her mother broiled, roasted, and sometimes made potpies with the game Annie brought home.[7]

The old Kentucky rifle that Annie's father had brought from Pennsylvania hung over the fireplace. The children were forbidden to use it. Annie had an uncontrollable curiosity about it. Many stories are told about her first experience shooting. She may have romanticized the story herself when she said, "I was eight years old when I took my first shot, and I still consider it one of the best shots I ever made. I saw a squirrel run down over the grass in front of the house, through the orchard and stop on a fence to get a hickory nut."[8] She ran into the house, climbed on a chair and slid the Kentucky rifle down to the mantle. She carried it outside, rested the barrel on the porch railing, and took aim. "It was a wonderful shot, going right through the head from side to side," she said.[9] That was the beginning of Annie's love of shooting.

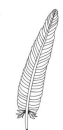

A Naughty Little Girl
Annie remembered:

> *It was because little mother did not think so much of little girls playing with guns, and because I just could not let that gun alone, that I did something very naughty—got the gun down from the rack behind the fireplace when mother was not looking and went out to practice.*[10]

Annie's mother tried to keep her family together. Jobs were scarce and did not pay much. To help support the family, she took care of sick people in their homes for $1.25 per week. The children were left home alone. During that time, families who made a comfortable living often offered to take an overburdened widow's children to raise with their own children. The neighboring Bartholomew family offered to take John and baby Hulda into their home until Mrs. Moses could care for them again.

Daniel Brumbaugh, whose wife had been dead several years, was a close neighbor. All his children were grown, and he was alone. He promised to take care of Mrs. Moses and her children if she would marry him. Susan Moses and Daniel Brumbaugh were married in August 1867. The family's happiness did not last long. Brumbaugh was in an accident and could not work. Annie's mother was left without any means of financial support.

Young Annie helped support her family by trapping and hunting. She later posed for this picture, wearing the same kind of clothing she had worn during her childhood.

Annie Leaves Home

After her stepfather's accident, ten-year-old Annie was sent to live with Samuel and Nancy Ann Edington, friends of Annie's mother. The Edingtons were superintendents of the Darke County Infirmary near Greenville. The infirmary was a home for orphans, the homeless, and the mentally handicapped. Annie was to earn her room and board by helping Mrs. Edington.

Mrs. Edington, a kind woman, wanted Annie to attend school with her son Frank, but Annie declined. She wanted to work as much as possible for extra money to send to her mother. She learned how to knit and how to use a sewing machine. She sewed, mended, and patched clothing for the infirmary inmates. In her spare time, she also learned how to make fancy embroidery.

Annie had been with the Edingtons a short time when the "he-wolf," as she always referred to him, came along. He wanted to hire a girl to watch his three-week-old son while his wife cared for their house and older children. He promised that she could go to school and continue to trap and shoot.[11]

Annie took the job believing the "he-wolf" would send her mother fifty cents a week for Annie's wages. When she got there, however, the situation was nothing like what the "he-wolf" had promised. Annie had to get up at four o'clock in the morning to cook breakfast, clean the kitchen, milk the cows and skim the cream from the milk, feed the cows and pigs, weed the garden, pick wild berries, prepare dinner, and care for the baby. In between, the "wolf" family, as she called them, expected her to trap and hunt.

"I was held a prisoner," she said. "They would not let me go."[12] The "she-wolf" kept Annie out of school and fed her poorly. She was also abused. One night, when Annie fell asleep while mending stockings, the "she-wolf" struck her and threw her out into the snow. She was almost frozen when the "he-wolf" returned home. Before he saw Annie in the snow, the wife grabbed her back inside the house and tried to warm her by the fire. Annie was very feverish during the night, and they let her rest the next day, but did not bring her food or drink.[13]

Annie suffered the "wolf" family's abuse for two years, thinking that they were sending her mother money. She was never told that her stepfather had died nor that her mother had written, begging her to come home. Her mother thought that Annie was being sent to school and was well treated and fed. One day when the "wolf" family was gone, Annie, age twelve, decided to run away.

Her loyalty to her mother and family had earned her many scars and bruises across her back. She was still no closer to knowing how to read and write than

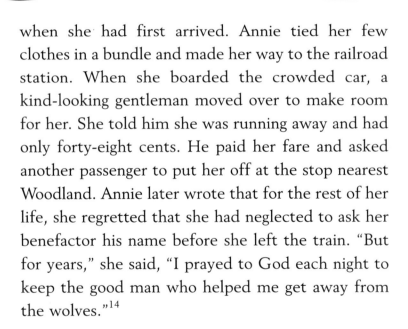

Child Labor

There were no child labor laws in the 1860s that protected children from being mistreated or forced parents to send their children to school. Often families took children into their homes and made them do all of the hard work. Abusive adults told the children they should be glad to have the chance to work for shelter and food.

when she had first arrived. Annie tied her few clothes in a bundle and made her way to the railroad station. When she boarded the crowded car, a kind-looking gentleman moved over to make room for her. She told him she was running away and had only forty-eight cents. He paid her fare and asked another passenger to put her off at the stop nearest Woodland. Annie later wrote that for the rest of her life, she regretted that she had neglected to ask her benefactor his name before she left the train. "But for years," she said, "I prayed to God each night to keep the good man who helped me get away from the wolves."[14]

3

A HAPPY BRIDE

Twelve-year-old Annie returned home to find that her mother was widowed again. Daniel Brumbaugh had died on November 4, 1870, leaving his wife with another daughter, Emily. Annie's three older sisters, Lydia, Sarah Ellen, and Elizabeth, were married. Still, Annie's mother had her three youngest children—Hulda, John, and Emily—living with her. The family was destitute again. Annie's mother could not afford to take care of Annie, now the oldest child at home.

Annie returned to the infirmary to live with the Edingtons, where she hoped to make extra money to help her mother. The Edingtons treated her like a daughter, and for a short time she attended school with their children. She was paid to sew dresses and make quilts for the people in the infirmary. She embroidered and stitched fancy cuffs and collars to brighten the orphans' dresses. Her jobs included milking the cows, saving the cream, and making butter for the kitchen.

She was so responsible in her jobs that the Edingtons gave her a raise. She began her lifelong habit of saving her earnings and sending her mother some money every payday. Money was more important to her than learning. After a few weeks of study, she dropped out of school to make as much money as possible.

She lived in fear that the "wolf" family would return to take her back to the farm. One day, the "he-wolf" burst into the infirmary schoolroom and demanded that Annie return with him. Mrs. Edington had seen bruises and welts on Annie's back from her stay with the "wolves." Her husband and sons threw the "he-wolf" out of the school and threatened to report him to the authorities if he returned. Annie later wrote, "That night I slept untroubled for the first time in long months."[1]

Just after Annie's fourteenth birthday, Annie's mother, "with two marriages of hardship and poverty behind her, . . . stepped into a third." When she married Joseph Shaw, another farmer, "the struggle began again to build a little home."[2]

Before their marriage, Joseph Shaw had sold his farm, intending to buy another one. A scoundrel cheated him out of all but five hundred dollars. He bought twenty-seven acres of land and hired a carpenter to build a small house. Shaw had to borrow money from the bank in order to buy the house. The bank had to be paid in regular payments, plus interest. "Grandpap," as the children called their new stepfather, delivered mail to Greenville, but he did not make enough money to pay off the mortgage.

Annie had been given a sixteen-gauge shotgun and a supply of ammunition.[3] However, she had no time and nowhere to hunt at the infirmary. She missed the outdoors and her solitary tramps through the woods. She also missed her family, who needed her. She decided to return home.

Susan Shaw, Oakley's mother, had a difficult life and depended on Oakley for financial help. Mrs. Shaw, a Quaker, instilled in Oakley a set of values that guided her through life.

Annie moved to the farm with her mother, now Susan Shaw, and her stepfather Joseph Shaw. Annie began hunting again.

A Good Businesswoman

On her way home from the Edingtons, she stopped in Greenville. Charles and G. Anthony Katzenberger had a grocery store on the town square. She knew that hunters traded their wild birds and game for staples such as flour, ammunition, traps, and harnesses. Annie wanted to trade her game for money and ammunition.[4]

The Katzenbergers had bought game from her before when she had trapped or shot more than her family could use. She worked out a deal with them. They agreed to market all the game she could furnish. From that day on, Annie earned her living with a gun.

Annie became a market hunter, a person who made money by selling game birds and furs. In later years when game limits were set, Annie was embarrassed when Charles Katzenberger showed her his old account books, listing the amount of game he had purchased from her. "I won't say how much, as I might be called a game hog," she said and never told the numbers or how much money she made.[5] She did say, "After the age of ten I never had a nickel in my pocket that I didn't earn."[6]

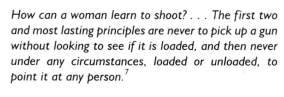

Lessons on Shooting

Annie Oakley explained her beliefs about the rules of shooting:

> *How can a woman learn to shoot? . . . The first two and most lasting principles are never to pick up a gun without looking to see if it is loaded, and then never under any circumstances, loaded or unloaded, to point it at any person.*[7]

Annie's hunting provided the money and food that the family needed. No one was more pleased than Mrs. Shaw when Annie gave her the money she had saved to pay the mortgage on the Shaw farm.[8]

With the mortgage paid, the family was secure at last. Now was the time for Annie to think about herself. Annie left her green fields and forest to find a greater adventure living with her sister and brother-in-law, Lydia and Joe Stein, in Cincinnati.[9]

According to family legend, Annie first heard the name Oakley while exploring Fairmount with Lydia Stein. The story was told that the two sisters were standing at the ridge of a steep street in Fairmount, when Lydia pointed to a suburban section of Cincinnati. "Joe and I almost moved to that part of the city, in Oakley or Hyde Park," she said. Annie liked the name and it stuck in her mind.[10]

Annie had never seen anything like Cincinnati. She had not realized that so many people could live so close together. Joe Stein took her to see big steamboats, driven by huge paddle wheels along the great bend of the Ohio River. She saw small canal boats drawn by mules plodding on the banks of the Miami Canal. She met adventurous pioneers moving

Annie Oakley paid off the mortgage on her mother's house, pictured here, by selling game to local businesses.

westward to begin a new life. She first discovered gun clubs and shooting galleries.

Until she went to Cincinnati, Annie had never shot a gun for entertainment. And she had not met a man like Frank Butler before.

A Future Husband

When Frank Butler came into Annie's life on Thanksgiving Day in 1875, Annie was just fifteen and he was twenty-five. He was a sharpshooter who made his living by giving shooting exhibitions. She was "just an unknown"[11] who made a living by shooting game. Butler was confident that he could outshoot a small girl even if she were "a crack shot from up country."[12] But Butler lost more than the prize money to Annie. He lost his heart.

Annie and Butler came from similar backgrounds. When Butler was eight years old, his impoverished parents left him with an aunt in Ireland. Planning to send for him later, they sailed from Ireland to the United States. He did not like the way his aunt treated him and ran away at the age of thirteen. He worked on the deck of a ship for his passage to the United States.

He was young and unskilled, but managed to support himself by doing odd jobs in New York City. He delivered milk with a pony cart, cleaned stables, and became a fisherman. He even tried to learn the glassblowing trade. He also learned to shoot.

Vaudeville acts—amateur theatrical groups— were popular during the 1870s. They appealed to Butler's sense of the dramatic, and he became a performer. He probably started performing between shows while workers changed the sets on stage. He did a trick-shooting act that became very popular because he was such an accurate shot. He could shoot while sighting through a mirror, and could fire a rifle while bending over backward. His most popular act was shooting an apple in half off the head of his poodle George.

Butler was a good-looking man. He was a little below average in height, with dark hair and a trim mustache. He liked to tell stories and play jokes on people. He was also sentimental and liked to write poetry.

Butler began to court Annie immediately after the contest that Thanksgiving Day. He gave Annie and her family tickets to his performance at the theater that night. After the show, Annie went backstage to meet George the poodle. George, who usually did not like women, became friends with Annie.

The next day, Annie sent a note to George. "George" responded with a box of candy. "George" wrote her letters and sent her small presents. Before

Almost fifty years after "George" courted Annie Moses, Annie Oakley and Frank Butler pose with their English setter, Dave. After George helped bring them together, their pets became an important part of their lives.

long, Butler stopped pretending to be George and began writing for himself. In less than a year, he asked Annie to marry him.

At first, Annie's mother disapproved of the engagement. Her Quaker principles opposed the kind of lifestyle Butler led. He was a sharpshooter in show business, and he was also divorced with a child. However, Annie's mother did like his easy-going personality, and the fact that he did not smoke, drink, or gamble. He quickly won her over with the loving way he cared for Annie.[13]

The wedding was simple. Annie wore a new gingham dress she had made. In later life, Annie wrote of her marriage to Butler, and George's role in the match: "Well, what fools we mortals be! If that poodle didn't lead me into signing some sort of alliance papers on Aug. 23, 1876 that tied a knot so hard it has lasted some fifty years."[14]

4

FIRST PUBLIC
APPEARANCE

Annie and Frank Butler had little money when they married. For several years, she spent much of her time at her mother's house while Butler traveled from one city to the next to perform. She passed the days practicing her reading and writing until she could finally write Butler letters on her own. Yet always the outdoors called to her.[1] She taught herself trick shooting by placing targets on fence posts. When she could, she joined Butler in his travels.

On May 1, 1882, she was with Butler in Springfield, Ohio, where he and his partner John Graham were to appear at the Crystal Hall Theater. Graham became ill and could not perform. It was decided that "Mrs. B." would go on stage and hold objects for "Mr. B." to shoot. "Mrs. B." rebelled. "No, I want to fire every other shot," she told him.[2]

Butler agreed. He took the first shot and hit the target. The audience groaned when "Mrs. B." missed her target. Most likely, she missed it on purpose to gain the sympathy of the audience.[3] She did not miss again. The audience stood up to applaud after she finished her last shot. She was a hit. The act was so successful that she joined Butler as his permanent partner.

When she became Butler's stage partner, she changed her name to Annie Oakley. Perhaps it was a name she remembered from her visit to Cincinnati, or maybe she just liked the way it sounded. Annie Oakley had a nice ring to it, and the name gave her an identity separate from her husband.

Oakley needed something other than street clothes to match her new name. Using skills she had learned at the infirmary years ago, she designed and made a costume out of material that looked like leather. She fashioned her own leggings to go with it. Her ankle-length skirt was shorter than the fashion during the late 1800s and early 1900s.

While she sewed, Butler read to her. He was patient in teaching her how to improve her reading and writing, as well as in teaching her all the stage

A Poet in the Family

The sentimental Frank Butler often wrote poetry. Here, he wrote about the change of seasons in Darke County:

> How do you do, Miss April
> I'm mighty glad you're here;
> Never did like old Miss March,
> She acts so very queer.[4]

tricks he could dream up. Practice, practice, practice, he told her—he was never satisfied.[5]

Oakley knew how to win over audiences. She sometimes missed the first shot so the rest of the show would be more dramatic. She ended each show with a little skip and kick, which became her trademark.

Oakley had a very feminine appearance. She wore her chestnut hair loose around her shoulders, flowing down her back. At five feet tall, she was petite and weighed just over a hundred pounds. She looked younger than her twenty-two years. Her "first gun of quality"—an 1878 Parker Brothers sixteen-gauge, double-barrel, breech-loading, hammer-mode shotgun—looked larger than she did.[6]

A Popular Act

As the Butlers traveled from city to city, their reputations grew. Audiences eagerly awaited their arrival. "Butler and Oakley" and their poodle

George became favorite specialty acts. George sat on a stool with an apple on his head. Either Butler or Oakley split the apple with a bullet. At the end of the act, George walked to the edge of the stage for his share of the applause.[7]

The Butlers traveled in railroad cars and stayed in theatrical boardinghouses, which were cheaper than hotels. Oakley never forgot her mother and sent her money every payday to help with expenses. They also began to save money.

Butler was always trying to improve their act by adding new tricks. Oakley shot the ashes off a cigarette being held in Butler's mouth. She hit a

Annie Oakley and a friend help a performing dog practice jumping.

dime held in his fingers and sliced a playing card in two. After clay pigeons were thrown into the air, she jumped over a table, picked up her shotgun, and hit the targets before they hit the ground.

Because of Butler's ability to think of new attractions, there was always work for them in vaudeville and stock companies. As they became better known, audiences knew they were in for a treat because Butler and Oakley were always improving their acts. The audience could always expect something different.

"Little Sure Shot"

As she became famous, Oakley had many admirers. Among the best known was Sitting Bull, chief of the great Sioux tribe. Sitting Bull was the leading elder and holy man of many of the tribes who fought

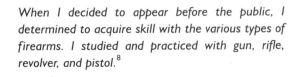

Appearing before the Public
Annie Oakley explained how she prepared for a career in show business:

> When I decided to appear before the public, I determined to acquire skill with the various types of firearms. I studied and practiced with gun, rifle, revolver, and pistol.[8]

against Lieutenant Colonel George Armstrong Custer and the 7th Cavalry at the Battle of the Little Bighorn. Custer and over two hundred soldiers had been killed in the battle.

Sitting Bull was in St. Paul, Minnesota, to take part in a ceremony celebrating the completion of the Northern Pacific Railroad in 1884 when he first saw Oakley. She and Butler were touring with the three-act play *Slocum's Oath*, which was then playing in the Olympic Theater in St. Paul. When Sitting Bull saw the play, he wanted to meet Oakley. He sent messages to her hotel, asking her to visit him. At first, Oakley just thought it was amusing and did not respond. She had an exhibition to think about.[9] Finally, Sitting Bull sent $65 and asked for an autographed picture of her. She returned the money with a picture and agreed to see him the next day. When she went to see him, he christened her *Watanya Cicilla*, or "Little Sure Shot," and insisted upon adopting her as his daughter.[10] It was the beginning of a very close friendship that would last for many years.

Butler and Oakley joined the Sells Brothers Circus in the spring of 1884. They had worked for the circus in 1883, too, but Oakley had appeared only as an equestrienne, or female horseback rider. In 1884, when the Butlers rejoined Sells Brothers, Oakley was billed as a markswoman. The season ended in New Orleans in November. People from all over the country had come to New Orleans to celebrate the one hundredth anniversary of America's first cotton export. The celebration was called the World's Industrial and Cotton Exposition.

Sells Brothers Circus set up tents on a lot just off Canal Street. The size of the audience varied with the weather. It often rained hard and was cold even under the canvas tents. After two weeks of losing money, the owners decided to close the circus and go home. Butler and Oakley were signed up for the next season, but they would be out of a job during the winter months.

Frank Butler, not one to waste time, placed an advertisement outlining their talents in the New York *Clipper*, a trade publication. While they were waiting for a response to the ad, Butler read a story about Buffalo Bill's Wild West. (Buffalo Bill Cody refused to call his Wild West a "show.")[11] The Wild West included horse races and shooting matches. Oakley had been trick-riding and shooting at the same time in the Sells Brothers Circus. Buffalo Bill's Wild West sounded ideal to the jobless couple.

Butler got no response from his advertisement, but during the last week of Sells Brothers Circus performances, William F. "Buffalo Bill" Cody visited the circus. Butler and Oakley met him and asked for a job. Unfortunately, Cody's show had lost money

Like Annie Oakley, Buffalo Bill Cody became a living symbol of the Wild West. During his lifetime, he was a military scout, a buffalo hunter, a Pony Express rider, and a world-famous showman.

during the past year and he could not afford to hire them. The show already had too many shooting acts, including the famous world championship shooter Captain Adam Bogardus and his four sons. Cody told them to look him up in Louisville, Kentucky, in the spring.

With the possibility of a job gone, Butler and Oakley packed up their belongings and headed north. They lived in theatrical boardinghouses and worked in variety theaters during the winter months. In March, they heard that Bogardus and his sons had left Buffalo Bill's Wild West.

Buffalo Bill's Wild West

Oakley wrote to Buffalo Bill immediately, and negotiations began between them. He felt Oakley was asking for too much money. He thought she was too small to have the strength to do the same kind of performance that Bogardus had done.[12]

Butler and Oakley proposed doing a three-day trial. If Cody was not pleased with her performance, they would leave the show with no questions asked. Cody liked the idea and invited them to Louisville, Kentucky, where the Wild West was opening during the last weekend in April 1885.

Because Butler had the ideas and the business knowledge and Oakley had better performing skills and more public appeal, Butler became Oakley's manager. He planned her act carefully, including some of her most daring tricks. Oakley spent most of April visiting with her family and practicing for her performance.

Oakley and Butler arrived at the park on the afternoon of the Wild West's opening. Thinking that everyone was at the opening day parade, Butler suggested that Oakley practice her act where it would take place. Oakley agreed, and began shooting. As she laid down her last gun, a man ran across the arena crying out, "Fine! Wonderful! Have you got photographs with your gun?"[13]

The man was Nate Salsbury, Buffalo Bill's partner. Impressed, he hired her on the spot, without a three-day trial. He then sent her to a photographer for new pictures with her gun.

After the parade on opening day, the cast of the Wild West lined up to meet Oakley. Buffalo Bill introduced her, saying, "This little Missy is

Posters were made to advertise Annie Oakley and Buffalo Bill's Wild West.

Annie Oakley. She is going to be shooting with us, and I want you boys to welcome her and treat her well."[14] From that day on, Cody always referred to Annie Oakley as "Missy."

Oakley later wrote, "There I was facing the real Wild West, the first white woman to travel with what society might have considered [an] impossible outfit." The Indian chiefs welcomed her with "How! *Washtay*!" meaning "All is good!" The rest of the traveling troupe followed their lead, and Oakley began seventeen years of being "just their little

Many artists tried to capture Annie Oakley and her horse in drawings. Oakley was as skilled shooting from horseback as she was standing still.

sister, sharing both their news of joy and sorrow from home."[15]

From her very first show, Oakley became a featured attraction, advertised as "The Peerless Wing and Rifle Shot." Mounted on her pony, she galloped from the shadows of the grandstand. Ringmaster Frank Richmond's excited voice filled the arena:

> Ladies and Gentlemen, the Honorable William F. Cody and Nate Salsbury present the feature attraction, unique and unparalleled, the foremost woman marksman in the world, in an exhibition of skill with the rifle, shotgun and pistol—the little girl of the Western Plains—Annie Oakley![16]

Wearing a fringed skirt and jacket with a wide-brimmed hat, Oakley opened fire. A cowboy riding ahead of her threw targets in the air. The roll of drums and the audience's applause filled the air as she shattered the targets. She jumped off her horse and ran to the center of the ring.

Butler threw glass balls in the air. Oakley vaulted over a table, grabbed a different gun, and shattered them before they hit the ground. She then took a mirror and turned her back on the target. Looking in the mirror at a target behind her, she placed a rifle on her shoulder and hit a small silver disk that Butler held over his head. The crowd roared as she jumped back on her horse and raced from the ring.

She became an overnight hit. The legend of Annie Oakley had begun.

5

BUFFALO BILL'S WILD WEST

Before Annie Oakley joined Buffalo Bill's Wild West, there had been no female featured performer. The entire production was a combination of rodeo drama, which romanticized life in the frontier West. Cowboys rode bucking broncos. Mexicans twirled lassos. American Indians beat tom-toms and went on the warpath. They burned a settler's cabin and ambushed the Deadwood Stage, an authentic stagecoach, which had been used by Blackhills Stage Line.

Buffalo Bill's Wild West was the creation of William Frederick Cody. Like Annie Oakley, Cody became a legend in his own time.

Born on February 26, 1846, Cody was always adventurous and saw no reason to stay in school after he had learned to read and write. Cody's father died when he was eleven. To help support his mother and sisters, Cody got a job as a delivery boy with a freight company. His first job away from home was as a driver for a wagon train. He herded the extra oxen and horses together and kept them out of the wagon's way. By the time he was fifteen, Cody was big and strong and an excellent rider. He convinced Captain Jack Slade to let him ride for the Pony Express. The job fit Cody's daring nature.

In 1867, he was hired for the job that earned him his nickname, "Buffalo Bill." Goddard Brothers, a company that supplied food to the construction crews of the Kansas Pacific Railroad, hired him to

The Pony Express
The Pony Express, a mail delivery service, started in 1860. A Pony Express rider changed horses every ten to twelve miles and rode seventy-five to one hundred miles a day at top speed. There were one hundred ninety stations, five hundred horses, and eighty riders. One of the first riders was Pony Bob Haslam, who later joined Buffalo Bill's Wild West.

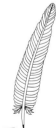

Cody Gets His Nickname

Whenever the workmen on the Kansas Pacific Railroad saw Cody coming with a load of buffalo meat, they chanted a jingle:

Buffalo Bill, Buffalo Bill
Never missed and never will
Always aims and shoots to kill
And the company pays his buffalo bill.[1]

kill twelve buffalo a day to provide meat for the crews. Cody later wrote that he killed 4,280 buffalo during his time with Goddard Brothers. Historians believe that number is an exaggeration.[2]

Cody was on a scouting expedition for the 5th Cavalry in 1869 when he met Edward Zane Carroll Judson, known as Ned Buntline. Buntline was an author of dime novels, which were cheap paperback books about adventure stories. Buntline wrote four books with Buffalo Bill as the central character. On December 23, 1869, *New York Weekly* published the first of a series titled *Buffalo Bill, the King of Border Men*. It was advertised as "The wildest and truest story [Buntline] ever wrote."[3] Actually, there was not much truth in the story, which was about Civil War border fighting. However, the Buffalo Bill legend began to grow as Cody was praised for his scouting skills.

Scouting brought Cody national fame in early 1872, when Grand Duke Alexis, son of the czar of Russia, visited the United States. His visit made headline news. General William Tecumseh Sherman, for whom Cody had been a scout, was taking the duke on a buffalo hunt. Sherman chose Cody to be their guide.

When he met the duke, Buffalo Bill was "dressed in a buckskin coat, trimmed with fur, and wore a black slouch hat, his long hair hanging in ringlets over his shoulders."[4] Newspapers described the meeting between Buffalo Bill and the duke, as well as every detail of the exciting hunt. Along with the duke of Russia, Buffalo Bill made newspaper headlines.

Show Business Calls

A new way of life began for Cody. In the fall of 1872, he and another scout and hunter—John Burwell Omohundro, Jr., known as Texas Jack—joined Ned Buntline in New York. Buffalo Bill played himself in Buntline's drama, *The Scouts of the Prairie.* For several years, Cody acted in melodramas in the fall and spring, and scouted in the summer. Over time, his acting became more and more of a western spectacle, and he began thinking about starting a "Wild West" show.[5]

Buffalo Bill's Wild West

Cody did not have enough money to start a company, so he formed a partnership with Dr. W. F. Carver, a sharpshooter. Cody and Carver had many disagreements and parted after several months. Cody then teamed up with actor Nate Salsbury and Captain Adam Bogardus, called the "Champion Pigeon Shot of America."[6] Together, they formed Buffalo Bill's Wild West.

By the time Annie Oakley joined the Wild West in 1885, the show's popularity had soared. Buffalo Bill had been the star attraction in the show, but that quickly changed. Although she had never been west of the Mississippi, Oakley became "the western girl." Because she played the role so well, she was an instant hit with the audience.

Oakley slipped into the routine of the traveling show as if she had done it all her life. The cast played one- and two-day stands throughout the eastern and central states and into Canada, performing in more than forty cities. They slept at night while the train traveled from one location to the next. They were up by five o'clock and ready to unload when the train stopped. The horses and buffalo were unloaded first and put in makeshift corrals where they could exercise and munch on hay.

Two tents were unloaded next and set up. One was for Cody and Salsbury, the other for Oakley and

Butler. The Butlers preferred the tent to staying in boardinghouses. It was furnished with a steamer trunk that opened up into a dresser, two folding chairs, two cots, a rug, and curtains for the door opening. They had hot water and a collapsible bathtub. Their food—"Everything in sight!"—was prepared by the troupe's cook, and the performers all ate together like a large family.[7]

"The travel and early parades were hard, but I was happy," Oakley later wrote.[8] She liked the show's people and they liked her. The audiences

The Butlers had their own tent when they traveled with the Wild West. Here, Annie Oakley reads in front of her tent at the Chicago World's Fair in 1893.

loved her. When she performed, she played to packed stands.

A Star Attraction

Oakley's act never grew mechanical or stale. When the drum rattled loud and fast and the bugles shrilled for attention, the Indians fell silent and the cowboys sat still in their saddles. All eyes turned toward the entrance to the arena as the ringmaster yelled, "Ladies and gentlemen, Miss Annie Oakley, the little girl of the Western Plains!"[9] Oakley rode into the arena as though she had just arrived from Fort Laramie or Deadwood City. Audiences stood and cheered her arrival.

Oakley's first few shots often brought squeals of fright from the women in the audience. The squeals quickly changed to round after round of applause. She set the audience at ease with her delicate looks and relaxed poise.

The first year with the Wild West was a happy one for Oakley and Butler, except for the death of their beloved dog George. The Wild West had arrived in Toledo, Ohio, in a downpour. The troupe had to walk from the train station to the show's camp. They had gone about a mile when George "just lay down and would go no further."[10] The Butlers took the dog in a cab the rest of the way, but George died that night.

Everyone knew how much Oakley loved George. The performers grieved with the Butlers. George was buried "in a private lawn" with "his pretty table cover under him and his beautiful satin and velvet cover with his name embroidered upon it over him."[11] Two cowboys lowered George's special-made coffin into the grave. The Indian women placed wreaths on the grave while they chanted death songs.

Sitting Bull Joins the Wild West

"Arizona John" Burke was the press agent and troubleshooter for Buffalo Bill's Wild West. Always on the lookout for attractions for the Wild West, Burke asked Sitting Bull to join the troupe. The chief refused until he learned that Annie Oakley, his adopted daughter, would be there.

Oakley welcomed Sitting Bull into the Wild West troupe, but audiences did not like him because his people

Sitting Bull, who performed with Buffalo Bill's Wild West in 1885, was very fond of Annie Oakley, and adopted her as his daughter.

had slaughtered Custer and his troops. When Sitting Bull appeared on stage, audiences hissed at him. A man in Philadelphia asked him if he had any regrets about the death of Custer and so many whites. Sitting Bull replied, "I have answered to my people for the Indians slain in that fight. The chief that sent Custer must answer to his people."[12]

During the months he traveled with the show, Sitting Bull and Oakley formed a strong friendship. At the end of the season, however, Sitting Bull decided to leave the Wild West and return to the reservation. He told a reporter, "The wigwam is a better place for the red man."[13]

The Butlers were glad to hear the band play "Auld Lang Syne" to mark the end of the touring season. They were free until the spring and went to Ohio to visit Oakley's mother. Oakley filled her days "going to school while [Butler] hunted quail, rabbit and squirrel."[14]

Annie Oakley, "Little Sure Shot" and "the little girl of the Western Plains," was already legendary.

6

NEW YORK'S FAVORITE ENTERTAINER

Annie Oakley was in for a surprise when she went to St. Louis, Missouri, to begin her second season with the Wild West. Without telling Oakley, Cody had hired two white women to join the show. One was a "society woman" who "thought it would be just 'too cute'" to see the world from "the back of a horse."[1] During the opening day parade, she had to be lifted from her horse. She quit and returned home that night. Oakley was pleased that the woman found "honest, hard work *just too cute.*"[2]

Oakley did not mind the society woman because she knew the woman would not last. Yet she was very unhappy about Lillian Frances Smith. Smith was a fifteen-year-old shooter from Coleville, California. When Smith reached the Wild West lot, she bragged that "Annie Oakley was done for" now that she had arrived.[3]

Oakley was the prettier of the two. She had more grace and poise and was a better shot. She was petite and had a "girl-next-door" look that the public loved. Oakley was also very competitive and had her career to protect. She dealt with the problem of Lillian Smith quickly and decisively. Since youth was an important part of her image, Oakley simply subtracted six years from her age. From the day after her twenty-sixth birthday, she began telling reporters she was born in 1866. She carried that story with her to the grave. She instructed her family not to put a date of birth on her tombstone.[4] Her rival, Lillian Smith, eventually left the Wild West in 1888.

The Wild West played in Boston, Baltimore, Washington, D.C., and Philadelphia. While they were in Washington, an insect flew into Oakley's ear. Butler poured oil into her ear to try to wash the insect out but it did not help. She went to a doctor in Philadelphia who found nothing in her ear. She began running a fever but kept working. The troupe settled at Erastina, a resort on Staten Island, for the rest of the season. Oakley went to another doctor who gave her a leech to put on her swollen ear.[5]

When she returned to the Wild West lot, she found the opening day parade lined up to take a chartered boat to New York City. Oakley and Buffalo Bill were to lead the parade. Thousands of spectators would be lined along the street to applaud and cheer. The parade meant everything to Oakley. She had made a new costume for it with matching accessories. She had embroidered the name "Oakley" on both sides of the cloth flaps decorating her horse. The outfit had cost a large sum of money.[6]

She told her groom to saddle her horse and ran to her dressing room. Within minutes, she was dressed in her new costume and flying through the gates to catch the parade half a mile away. She reached the boat on time and rode in the seventeen-mile parade. Thousands of people cheered as she waved and blew kisses to those lining the streets.

Following the parade, Butler had to lift Oakley off her pony. She was too weak to walk. As soon as she was put to bed in their tent, Butler applied the leech to her ear and a stream of blood spurted out. She bled for five hours. The next day, a doctor pierced her ear to drain the infection and said that she had blood poisoning. Oakley recovered after

staying in bed for four days. It was the only time she missed a performance in forty years.

Sharpshooter Skills Challenged

During the later part of the season, Oakley was challenged by some of the best shots in the world. She began to shoot for money and prizes. She agreed to shoot three matches against the English champion, William Graham. Graham had come to America to try to beat the sharpshooters with the best reputations.

Oakley put up $100 to enter the first match and was guaranteed 75 percent of the gate receipts. She knew that Graham would be a challenge. Before the match, Oakley practiced with a new gun. She asked Butler to try it out to see if it shot accurately. Just as she slid a target into the trap, the spring released and cut her left hand. She had to have five stitches and was told not to use the hand for two weeks.

Butler wanted to postpone the match. Graham's manager wanted Oakley to forfeit so he and Graham would get all of the money. Oakley refused to forfeit the match. On October 8, 1886, she was the first to shoot. The live birds were fast, and she had to use her wounded left hand to raise the gun. On her first shot, three of the stitches ripped open. Butler stopped the match, so Graham got the $100.

Butler announced that 75 percent of their admission tickets would be refunded to the spectators. Annie Oakley lost the prize money, but she won the approval and cheers of the crowd.[7]

Oakley always got good press releases. Between Butler's press-agent skills and her own showmanship, Oakley was responsible for the best publicity the Wild West received while they were on Staten Island. One Sunday when she was out riding, she discovered an orphanage. Memories of her days in the infirmary came rushing back to her. She would never forget how poor she had been and how hard she had worked.

She talked to the director of the orphanage and invited the children to the show as her guests. The next day, fifty orphans arrived. Oakley escorted

Oakley Does Well, for a Woman
Reporters always had positive things to say about Annie Oakley, like this statement from a 1913 newspaper:

> *[Annie Oakley] has made a proud record by her wits, her activity, her genius, her naturalness, her brightness of mind, her courteous nature and her bravery.*
> *What more could you ask, especially of a woman!*[8]

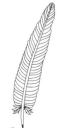

them around and paid for popcorn, ice cream, and pink lemonade. She had reserved a special section for them to watch the show. The children sat wide-eyed and spellbound as Buffalo Bill and Annie Oakley, followed by American Indians and cowboys, filled the arena.[9]

John Burke, never one to miss a press opportunity, sent free tickets to every orphanage in New York City for "Annie Oakley Day." The publicity that it generated ensured a full house at every performance for the rest of the summer. Yet more important to Oakley than the publicity were the happy smiles of the children.[10]

New York City loved Annie Oakley and she loved it.[11] The largest city in America, it glittered with electric lights in the hotels, restaurants, and theaters. Trains drawn by steam locomotives roared above the city streets on elevated tracks, whisking people from one part of town to another with breathtaking speed. Below, the streets were jammed with slower-moving horsecarts. Right in the middle of all that excitement was Madison Square Garden.

More New Acts

After the summer season was over, the Wild West, with all its equipment, animals, and employees, moved to Madison Square Garden. There, Cody introduced a new four-act show called "The Drama of Civilization" on the day before Thanksgiving, 1886. At the first performance, "fully 6,000 people were present and the whole circle of boxes was gay with men and women in evening dress."[12]

Oakley was ready for the occasion. She had been practicing new stunts. First, she did her usual target shots to get the audience used to the sound of guns firing. Then, she tied a handkerchief around her horse's leg just above the hoof. Riding sidesaddle at full speed, she leaned down and untied the handkerchief. "She and many others believe that this was never before done from a sidesaddle by anything in the semblance of a woman," reported the New York *Clipper*.[13]

A New Jersey newspaper reported, "It seemingly makes no difference to her whether she sits upright on the horse, lies extended, or faces forward or backward. Her shots from under a horse's neck made with the animal on a run would cause a Comanche to turn green with envy."[14] The Ladies Riding Club of New York was so impressed that its members gave Oakley a gold medal.[15]

Fake Annie Oakleys

After almost a year in New York, Annie Oakley had become so popular that people began copying her. One day, Butler saw a longhaired man posing as a cowboy and his female companion posing as "Little

Sure Shot." Butler was so angry he wrote to a newspaper, "The fact that she was about a foot taller than the original 'Little Sure Shot' made no difference to her."[16]

Butler also appealed to a number of sporting magazines to let him know if there were any reports of other fake Annie Oakleys. Just before the cast of the Wild West left New York for London, he took out an ad in the New York *Clipper*. In big, bold letters, the ad read: "DON'T FORGET THIS. There is only one Annie Oakley and she leaves for Europe with the Wild West."[17]

The Wild West was about to sail for London to help celebrate Queen Victoria's Golden Jubilee, the fiftieth anniversary since she was crowned. All over England there would be celebrations with the

Oakley's Peculiarities

Newspapers reported every detail about Annie Oakley and her performances:

> All great people have little physical peculiarities. When Miss Annie Oakley misses her aim she stomps her foot upon the ground; when she hits she kicks— a decided, unmistakeable kick.[18]

largest in London, the British capital and the largest city in the world in 1887.

While Butler took care of business, Oakley returned to Darke County to visit her mother, whom she had not seen for several months. Her mother was still having a difficult time, although her life had improved over the years with the money Oakley sent. However, Oakley's eighty-five-year-old stepfather, Joseph Shaw, was blind and near death. Oakley knew it would not be long before her mother was alone again. It was a sad parting when she left to return to New York. She "kissed the tears from [her] mother's eyes when she said goodbye."[19]

Four days later, the Wild West left New York on a special steamer for London. The girl from Darke County was going to perform before kings and queens.

7

A HIT IN LONDON

Annie Oakley was going to Europe as a messenger of goodwill to all the world. The Wild West was to show the European people the American way of life as the pioneers had known it.

On the voyage to London, the ship sailed into a storm. The ship's propeller was smashed and for forty-eight hours, the ship bounced and drifted in the rough sea. Everyone in the Wild West company was seasick except for Oakley. She was having the adventure of a lifetime. By the time the sea grew calm again, the ship had drifted 246 miles off its course. Oakley later learned that it was on the worst day of the storm that her stepfather had died.

After eleven days at sea, their ship, the *State of Nebraska*, arrived in England, much to everyone's relief. As the ship moved up the Thames River, the troupe saw posters of Buffalo Bill, Annie Oakley, American Indians, and cowboys plastered on buildings. Curious Londoners ran along the river to wave at the group. The London *Times* described the novelty of the troupe in England, "the like of which has never before crossed the seas."[1]

On May 6, 1887, before the show officially opened, there was a command performance for Prince Edward, son of Queen Victoria and future king, his wife, Princess Alexandria, and their children. Oakley later said, "We all worked like little hound dogs at a rabbit hole."[2]

The work paid off. Oakley shot so well the prince called her to the royal box where he and the princess were seated. When Oakley was introduced to them, the prince held out his hand. She ignored him and shook Princess Alexandria's hand first. "You will have to excuse me, please," she said to the prince, "because I am an American and in America, ladies come first."[3]

Oakley had been told that her success or failure in London depended on one critic who wrote under the name "Pen Dragon." He was said to be merciless, but fair. The morning after opening night, she read his review of the performance. Her "merciless"

Oakley Is the Subject of a Sermon

A London newspaper reported that a local minister, the Reverend Doctor Scudder, used Annie Oakley as the subject of his sermon. He said, "If you will all aim as straight for Heaven as Annie Oakley does at objects she shoots at, you can all be 'Little sure shots' and will all go to Heaven."[4]

critic had written, "It was a relief when Annie Oakley appeared. Somehow the vast audience expected to see something and they were not disappointed, for she shattered the flying missiles with precision and dramatic effect."[5]

The Wild West was a hit from its first day in England. In the first three weeks of May, the show attracted half a million visitors. Buffalo Bill and Annie Oakley had begun what were to become fifteen years of popularity in London.

Oakley was lauded with praise and showered with gifts. So many flowers were sent to her tent that she could not keep them all. She sent most of them to the women's and children's hospital wards in the Jubilee Memorial Hospital.

The Queen, Tea, and Blue Rocks

On May 12, the Wild West gave its second command performance for royalty. Queen Victoria and her royal party came in carriages from Windsor Castle.

Annie Oakley displays the many medals she won during her years of touring and performing in sharpshooting contests all over the world.

The queen was impressed with Oakley's performance. When Oakley was presented to her, Queen Victoria said, "You are a very clever little girl."[6] The encounter was published in newspapers worldwide. While it was good publicity for the Wild West, it was even better for Annie Oakley.

She became so popular in London that she was recognized everywhere she went. There were many receptions and teas given in her honor. Her costumes were copied by fashion houses and became popular among sportswomen. Oakley became the first woman ever invited to visit two elite gun clubs: the London Gun Club at Notting Hill and the Hurlingham Club on the banks of the Thames River.

It was at the London Gun Club that she first tried shooting at English pigeons. Blue rocks, pigeons found in England, were different from those in America. Small and very fast, blue rocks were raised especially for live-bird matches. They were also very expensive at five dollars a dozen.

Oakley used an American gun "all bedecked with gold, showing a gold figure of [herself] set in the guard."[7] The gun weighed seven and a half pounds and had too much drop. The four-inch drop caused her to shoot under the birds. As pretty as it was, the gun was not the best for "those little blue streaks of birds that made for the high stone wall like greased lightning."[8]

Oakley's score was unusually poor. She hit only five blue rocks out of twenty. After the exhibition, she was introduced to J. H. Walsh, editor of the *London Field*. Walsh was considered an expert on shooting. He greeted her by saying, "Miss Oakley, I expected to meet a much better shot but not so much a lady."[9]

Special Firearms for Oakley

When Oakley shot her first match at the London Gun Club, she owned three sixteen-gauge hammer guns. They were good guns for that time, but were not made to fit her small shoulder. Charles Lancaster, one of London's best-known gun makers, had seen Oakley's exhibition. He had a reputation for fitting a gun to a specific person and for improving rifle barrels.

With Oakley's permission, Lancaster improved her gun by straightening the stock. He also thought the gun was too heavy for her. He set about making a new, much lighter one. When he finished the twelve-gauge, double-barreled shotgun, she said, "The fit is perfection."[10]

Lancaster predicted that Oakley would kill thirty-five out of fifty blue rocks before she left England. He set up a match at his shooting grounds on September 30. That day, Oakley killed forty-one of fifty birds. She had conquered the English pigeons.[11]

As her popularity soared, Oakley began to receive marriage proposals. Since Butler was always in the background as her manager, few people knew he was her husband. She was referred to in the press as "Miss Oakley." Although she was twenty-seven, most people thought she was about twenty years old and unmarried. The Butlers did not tell the real story because Oakley's youthful image seemed to increase her popularity. If Frank Butler ever felt threatened or jealous, he never showed it.[12]

One of the proposals Oakley received was from a French count who watched her act every day for a month. He finally wrote her a letter declaring his undying "devotion."[13] He promised they could "spend his worldly goods,"[14] which were many. All she had to do was to write *yes* and he would arrange a proper introduction.[15]

Frank Butler answered the letter, informing the count of their marriage. One of Oakley's nieces, Annie Fern Swartwout, said she often heard her uncle Frank tease, "I wish I had let the Frenchman have you." Oakley usually replied kiddingly, "I wish you had, too!"[16]

Another proposal that Oakley frequently told about was from a Welshman who signed his letter, "Yours until death do us part, your Darling Ducky."[17] He also enclosed his photograph. Oakley said, "If I had been 80, [and] toothless . . . , I could not have said 'Yes' after one look at that pointed chin."[18]

Not all of Oakley's time in London was spent performing with the Wild West. Never one to miss an opportunity to make money, she did many shooting exhibitions. Financially, she had a successful six months, making as much as $750 extra in one week. Besides sending money to her mother, Oakley gave to charity, particularly for mothers and children. Always in the back of her mind were her early days of poverty.

The American Exhibition closed at the end of Queen Victoria's Jubilee in late October 1887. The Wild West then moved from London to Manchester, England. Oakley and Butler were not with them. They had quit the Wild West. Neither Cody nor the Butlers ever said why they quit. Oakley's only comment on the break was: "The reasons for doing so take too long to tell."[19]

Annie Oakley posed for this formal portrait around 1900. A friend's daughters are pictured in her brooch.

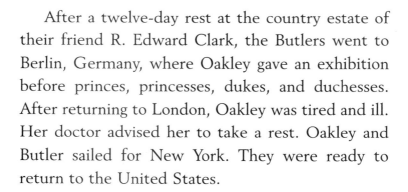

God's Own Country

When Oakley returned to the United States at the end of the London tour, she was asked how she liked Europe. She changed the question to "How did I like England?" She answered:

> First rate, indeed, except for the climate. . . . But, as you know, there is only one United States and to me it is God's own country.[20]

After a twelve-day rest at the country estate of their friend R. Edward Clark, the Butlers went to Berlin, Germany, where Oakley gave an exhibition before princes, princesses, dukes, and duchesses. After returning to London, Oakley was tired and ill. Her doctor advised her to take a rest. Oakley and Butler sailed for New York. They were ready to return to the United States.

8

A HIT IN PARIS

Annie Oakley and Frank Butler returned to New York. They arrived to a winter wonderland on Christmas Eve in 1887. As soon as they came off the ship, they took a taxi to Madison Square. They settled into a cozy apartment for the winter.

While Oakley rested, Butler stayed busy as her manager. He was a shrewd businessman. He had several ideas about how to keep Oakley's name in the press. Annie Oakley had become very well known, but the public was fickle about entertainment stars. Her name had to be kept in the press or she would soon be forgotten. Also, they had to have an income or they would soon spend all their savings.

Butler placed ads in the New York *Clipper* announcing that Annie Oakley was to star in a new melodrama called *Little Sure Shot, the Pony Express Rider*. He also said Oakley would welcome the assistance of a financial backer.[1]

While they waited for responses to their ads, Butler arranged a series of shooting matches for Oakley. If she won, they could easily pick up a few hundred dollars. William Graham, the British champion, asked for three matches. Graham wanted to take up where they had left off when Oakley had injured her hand. When the first match took place at a New Jersey racetrack, it was bitterly cold, with blowing sleet. Oakley lost the match, thirty-six to thirty-three.

The second match with Graham was two weeks later in Easton, Pennsylvania. When Oakley and Butler arrived at their hotel, they were put in room thirteen. Her superstitious fans begged her to change rooms. They threatened to change their bets if she did not. She stayed in the room and won the match.

The third and final match was held back in New Jersey. This time, Oakley requested room thirteen. The bets were three to one against her. Oakley later said that Graham "tried in every conceivable way, that his little . . . head, could think of to get me rattled, so I would miss. But I was serene and just concentrated on my five traps and the score was 45–47 in my favor."[2] Graham offered fifty dollars to any man there who could match her shot for shot. There were no takers. Oakley had defeated the champion shooter of England.

Earning Extra Money

There were many other exhibitions and matches. Oakley played in vaudeville theaters with Tony Pastor's company. She began to set shooting records. One day, in three minutes and ten seconds, she shattered 100 glass balls out of 109 thrown in the air. She defeated the well-known shooter, Phil Daly, Jr., at his own tournament in New Jersey. At the Boston Gun Club in Wellington, Massachusetts, she hit two half-dollars in the air.

Oakley was performing with Pastor's company in Brooklyn when Buffalo Bill's Wild West returned to New York on May 21, 1888. Thousands of admirers waited on the docks to greet the cast. Buffalo Bill bowed and waved his hat. He spoke highly of the English people. Annie Oakley's name was not mentioned.

She did not help her relationship with Cody by signing up with a rival company. Another arena show, Comanche Bill's Wild West, offered her three hundred dollars a week and hotel expenses for both Oakley and Butler. The offer was top dollar for

Annie Oakley shot in more than one thousand contests and exhibitions. She set many records, some of which still stand.

the day. Unfortunately, Butler signed the contract before checking on the company.

When he did check, he found the show to be poorly operated and equipped. There was a string of half-wild Texas ponies, a camp of sullen Comanches, and a group of pseudocowboys who had never ridden a bronco.

"It won't do, Missy," Butler told Oakley. "I can't afford to have you connected with a failure."[3]

Butler was on his way to cancel the contract with Comanche Bill when he read in the paper that Pawnee Bill's Historical Wild West Exhibition and Indian Encampment was broke and stranded in Pittsburgh. The show's owner, Gordon W. Lillie, who called himself Pawnee Bill, had once traveled with Buffalo Bill's Wild West. Butler knew he was a hardworking and honest young man.[4]

With Butler's help, Comanche Bill and Pawnee Bill joined together to present Pawnee Bill's Wild West. Crowds lined the streets to watch the opening day parade. Pawnee Bill and Annie Oakley led the parade, followed by Pawnee, Comanche, Kiowa, Kaw, and Wichita Indians, cowboys, trappers, hunters, and scouts. Oakley wore her prettiest costume, topped by her trademark western hat with one side of the brim clipped with a star. The crowds cheered as she pranced by on her pony.

Setting Shooting Records

"There is but one Annie Oakley, and she is with us," read Pawnee Bill's advertisements.[5] Oakley lived up to expectations. On July 31, 1888, before twenty thousand people, she broke her own record by shooting forty-nine out of fifty live pigeons. She was a star again and loved by the press. When the successful season closed, it was a sad parting for both the Butlers and Pawnee Bill.[6]

Oakley returned to Tony Pastor's company in New York. Butler stayed busy scheduling interviews, exhibitions, and matches for his wife. Her shooting matches kept her name before the public.

Bold print headlines announced: "BEATEN BY A GIRL Miss Oakley outshoots Fred Knoll—She was modest about it." The reporter ended the article by saying: "It must be said in Mr. Knoll's favor that he did some very good shooting. All his birds acted badly."[7]

Another headline reported: "MISS OAKLEY BREAKS RECORD." The article read: "Miss Annie Oakley, the famous trap-shot, broke all records at a double clay-pigeons on Tuesday. . . . Annie Oakley hit a perfect score of 50. The referee, Frank McQuade, pronounced Annie Oakley's shooting the most remarkable he had ever seen."[8]

By the end of 1888, Oakley had set an American record at doubles by scoring twenty-five pairs of birds in a row. She defeated New Jersey state champion Miles Johnson, who reportedly had never been beaten on New Jersey soil. Oakley missed her forty-seventh bird, "a blue twister who went from No. 5 trap like a rocket."[9] Oakley turned to Johnson and said, "Did you bring that bird from England?" "No," he replied. "I trained that fellow to get one miss on you."[10]

On December 22, Oakley appeared in the first dramatic role written for her. *Deadwood Dick, or the Sunbeam of the Sierras*, was billed as "the greatest and most thrilling border drama ever produced."[11] Reviews of the play were enthusiastic about her shooting skill but did not mention her acting ability. "She [Annie Oakley] is justly styled the 'Queen of the Rifle,' and her wonderful skill as a 'markswoman' makes the spectator look upon the petite and graceful creature in open-eyed amazement. . . . Her aim seems to be unerring."[12]

Another Tour With Buffalo Bill

In spite of good reviews, *Deadwood Dick, or the Sunbeam of the Sierras*, closed on the last day of January 1889. By March, rumors were flying that Annie Oakley was going to join another Wild West company. Buffalo Bill Cody and Nate Salsbury were annoyed at her popularity. Salsbury called on the Butlers to tell them he would "fight any company that [Oakley] joined."[13]

"You cannot afford to fight my wife," Butler told him.[14]

Just as there are no records of why Oakley left the Wild West, there are no records to explain why she joined them again. Details of the verbal contract were

The Way to Success
Annie Oakley described her attitude about reaching for a goal and becoming successful:

> Aim at a high mark and you'll hit it. No, not the first time, nor the second time, and maybe not the third. But keep on aiming and keep on shooting for only practice will make you perfect. Finally, you'll hit the bull's eye of success.[15]

never revealed. Buffalo Bill's Wild West was preparing for another European tour. Oakley had been very popular before. Perhaps Cody and Salsbury were afraid of losing some of the show's appeal. For whatever reason, Cody and Oakley settled their differences and remained friends for the rest of their lives.

With just a month left before going abroad, the Butlers returned to Ohio for a visit. They knew it would be several years before they saw their family again. Oakley's mother was comfortable in the remodeled house made possible by the money Oakley sent her. Two nieces and one nephew had been added to the family. Because the Butlers had no children of their own, they showered attention on Oakley's sisters' children. Neighbors came to see Oakley and to watch her practice. She was the only celebrity they knew.

After a pleasant visit in Ohio, the Butlers were ready to sail on April 12, 1889. *The Persian Monarch*, with the whole company on board, including animals and equipment, headed toward the port of Le Havre, France. Once the ship docked, everything was loaded in freight cars and taken to Paris, where the Paris Universal Exposition was to be held. France was celebrating the one hundredth anniversary of the start of the French Revolution.

The Wild West found that the French people were not as warm as the English had been. The show

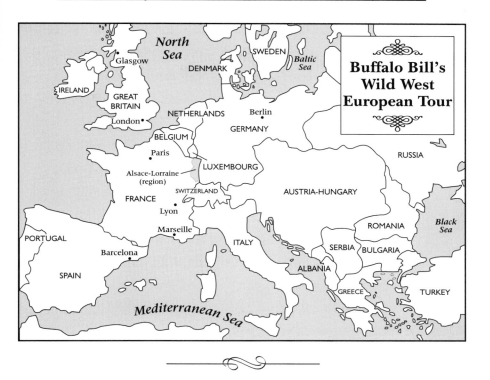

Buffalo Bill's Wild West successfully toured Europe twice. This map shows some of the cities in which the Wild West performed during its European travels.

was a curiosity from the day it opened in May 1889. Except for two French-Canadians, no one in the Wild West spoke French.

The first dress rehearsal was performed before the French president and his wife, Madame Carnot, and several thousand prominent Parisians. The audience was not familiar with American history. They did not understand the show. They sat aloof with little applause, even though they had "clackers" to lead them. It was the custom in foreign countries for clackers, who stood at each corner of the reserved seats, to begin the applause. When Butler saw them, he told them to sit down. Oakley "wanted honest applause or none at all."[16]

When Oakley bounded into the arena, there was no applause. "They sat like icebergs at first," she wrote. "There was no friendly welcome, just a 'you must show me' air."[17] And show them she did. It was not long before the audience was on its feet yelling "Bravo!" At the end of her act, she "bowed to the roaring handkerchief throwing mad 20,000."[18]

Annie Oakley, the little girl from Darke County, Ohio, had taken Paris by storm.

9

A
SOPHISTICATED
LADY

Annie Oakley's popularity grew with the publicity in the Paris newspapers. She turned down an offer from the president of France to be commissioned in the French army. She also refused to be sold to the king of Senegal for one hundred thousand francs. The king wanted her to go to Senegal and shoot all of the man-eating tigers. She and Butler refused his offer and went with the Wild West when it left Paris to tour southern France.

Oakley and Butler were honored in Marseille and Lyon with invitations to join in pigeon shoots. Butler collected the money, and Oakley collected the medals. From France, the troupe sailed on to Barcelona, Spain.

The visit to Barcelona was a mistake. The city was stricken with Spanish flu, typhoid, and small-pox. Over half the Wild West camp became ill. Ringmaster Frank Richmond died of the flu. Four American Indians died of smallpox. Butler and Oakley both "had the flu in earnest."[1] The company was quarantined for weeks, before they could move on to tour Italy, Switzerland, Germany, and Austria.

After touring Europe, they moved their winter camp to Alsace-Lorraine, France. The Butlers left the camp for England to visit old friends. Cody returned to the United States for the off-season.

It was late December when Oakley and Butler read a startling newspaper headline: "Annie Oakley Dead." The article said she had died of congestion

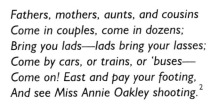

Advertisement for the Wild West
A Glasgow, Scotland, paper was so enthusiastic about the Wild West that it encouraged its readers to attend the performances:

> Fathers, mothers, aunts, and cousins
> Come in couples, come in dozens;
> Bring you lads—lads bring your lasses;
> Come by cars, or trains, or 'buses—
> Come on! East and pay your footing,
> And see Miss Annie Oakley shooting.[2]

of the lungs in Buenos Aires, Argentina. Newspapers all over the world had picked up the story.

Cody, reading the article in the United States, immediately sent three cables to Butler. Butler quickly wired back: "Annie just finished a full Christmas platter. No truth in report." Cody replied: "I am so glad our Annie ain't dead, ain't you?"[3]

Although Oakley saw humor in the situation, she worried that her mother might have spent days grieving her death. Butler and Oakley wrote hundreds of letters thanking people for their kind words upon reading the death notice. Butler wrote many news releases similar to the one he sent to the editor of *Shooting and Fishing*:

> The Paris papers of Dec. 28, published the obituary of Miss Oakley, saying she died of congestion of the lungs. There is only one consolation in reading this notice, the papers speak so very highly of her. . . .
>
> Frank Butler
> Ashford England Dec. 31, 1890

The confusion had been caused by the death of Annie Oatley, an American singer.

Another European Tour

Very much alive and healthy, Annie Oakley joined the Wild West for a second tour in Europe in April 1891. By the time the Wild West returned to New York in October 1892, Annie Oakley was a sophisticated woman of the world. Her travels in

Europe had taught her much more about culture, geography, and politics than she could have learned in school. However, her polished, ladylike demeanor did not keep her from being the first to run down the gangplank when the *Mohawk* docked. Oakley was excited to be back in America.[4]

The press in the United States had not forgotten Annie Oakley. She was interviewed by several newspapers in New York. She was grateful for the interviews. She said, "I guess the press had made me famous. But you know, some really peculiar things have been said."[5] The false reports of her death and another report that she had become engaged to an Englishman could be laughed away, and even Oakley did not correct some of the stories that romanticized her childhood. Though sometimes the reports were inaccurate, there had never been uncomplimentary remarks made about her.

While preparations were being made for the opening of the Wild West's 1893 season, the Butlers rushed to Ohio to visit Oakley's family. Oakley displayed all her medals for family and neighbors to see. A long clothesline was stretched outside, and Oakley's costumes were hung out to air. Oakley, her mother, and her sister Hulda spent days getting her costumes ready for another season. Some were discarded, some were mended, and new ones were made. After everything was done, the costumes were pressed and packed in tissue paper for the next season.[6]

A Home in Nutley

After their rest in Ohio, the Butlers settled into a hotel in New York. They began looking for a house to buy. An ad offering land for sale in Nutley, New Jersey, just fourteen miles from New York, caught their eyes. Nutley was an old town with a stream flowing through it. It was a quiet place where many artists and writers lived. The Butlers bought a corner lot and set a builder to work.

While the house was being built and the Wild West was preparing for the World's Fair in Chicago, Oakley and Butler stayed busy. They had used much of their savings for the house and had no steady income. Butler went to work as an agent for Remington Arms Company, selling guns. Oakley gave exhibitions in gun clubs and drill halls. In February 1893, she was the star at Tony Pastor's Opera House. During that time, she also practiced on her new bicycle for the Wild West opening in Chicago.

"The White City," where the Chicago World's Fair was to be held, was built for the occasion. Fair officials refused to let the Wild West set up within the fair gates because they felt it lacked dignity. Cody went across the street to Jackson Park and leased fourteen acres. Buffalo Bill's Wild West and

After Annie Oakley learned to do tricks on a bicycle, she was paid to do bicycle advertisements. She designed and made her own riding costumes.

Congress of Rough Riders of the World, as the show was now being called, opened on April 26, 1893, five days before the fair.

The Chicago World's Fair brought the Wild West to the height of its fame. It played to thousands of people every day during the 186-day season and made a record income of $1 million. Dressed in one of her thirty-five costumes, Oakley was first on the program after the Grand Review. Her success soared with that of the Wild West. She became one of the best-known women in America.[7]

The Butlers' Nutley home was completed in December. They moved in just before Christmas in 1893.

The First Movie Studio

In 1892, inventor Thomas Edison applied for a patent on his kinetograph, a movie camera, and his kinetoscope, a movie viewer for one person. He built the first movie studio on a swivel mechanism that revolved to catch the best sunlight for filming.

In May 1894, Edison gathered many stars in West Orange, New Jersey, to perform before his movie camera. Annie Oakley was filmed as she performed the shooting feats that had made her famous.

Several kinetoscopes were placed in a store. Each had a film on a different subject to tempt viewers to see all of them. People lined up to see the movies, which ran ninety seconds and cost a nickel. A new era of entertainment had begun.

In 1893, the American economy fell into a depression. Times were hard. When the Wild West opened on May 12, 1894, at Ambrose Park, Brooklyn, New York, there was no big crowd like usual. People could not afford to spend money on entertainment. That year, operating costs far exceeded income for the Wild West. When the show closed on October 6, it was the last time the show stayed in one location for an entire season.

With the closing of the Wild West, Oakley and Butler sailed for England. They took with them Oakley's horse, Gypsy, and twelve foxhounds to be used in her new play, *Miss Rora*. The play, written especially for her, received good reviews. The Hereford *Times* called her "a superb HORSEWOMAN" and "a LITHESOME ACTRESS . . . completely enthralled with her part."[8]

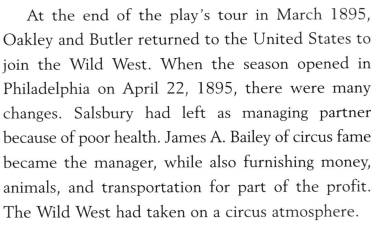

The End of the American Frontier
The year 1890 was a turning point in American history. The United States Census Bureau announced the end of the American frontier, saying that the continent had been settled from coast to coast. Many commentators complained that the age of the telephone, steam turbine, internal combustion engine, electric elevator, and hand camera was corrupting the United States. Some predicted the decline of American civilization.

At the end of the play's tour in March 1895, Oakley and Butler returned to the United States to join the Wild West. When the season opened in Philadelphia on April 22, 1895, there were many changes. Salsbury had left as managing partner because of poor health. James A. Bailey of circus fame became the manager, while also furnishing money, animals, and transportation for part of the profit. The Wild West had taken on a circus atmosphere.

In 190 days, Wild West gave 131 performances and traveled more than 9,000 miles. It took fifty-two railroad cars to transport personnel, animals, and equipment from town to town.

For over two years, the Butlers were on the road. They traveled with the Wild West and visited Ohio during their breaks. Oakley took part in many exhibitions and matches. Butler continued to work as an agent for gun manufacturers. Despite their different jobs, they found they could not keep up their house in Nutley. For a while they rented it, but eventually sold it at a loss.

The Butlers, as well as Cody, often talked about retiring. They were tired of traveling. "I have thought several times I would not go with the show another year, but I always do," Oakley said in 1899.[9] The choice was eventually made for her.

On October 28, 1901, the troupe boarded the three-sectioned train to go to Virginia for their last performance of the season. At 3:20 A.M., a southbound freight collided with the second section of the train in which the Butlers were sleeping.

Many Annie Oakley legends began with that accident. One rumor was that her "right hip was torn away."[10] Another was that she suffered severe nerve damage. Various accounts said Oakley needed surgery, was hospitalized for several months, was paralyzed on her left side, or that she needed a cane to help her walk. Still another said that her beautiful dark brown hair had turned white in seventeen hours.[11] Oakley biographers have questioned both the injuries and the hair color change. On one point, however, all the stories agree. It was the end of Oakley's career with Buffalo Bill's Wild West.

THE LAST
SHOW

Reports of the train accident spread worldwide. The *American Field* happily reported that Annie Oakley received only two slight injuries, one on the hand and one on the back.[1] By December 17, Oakley was accepting challenges to take part in shooting matches. It was at a match on January 16, 1902, that the New York *Sun* first noticed her white hair.

For the first time, youthful Annie Oakley looked older than her forty-one years. Oakley's friend Amy Leslie claimed that Oakley's hair had turned white after a careless attendant had left her in a scalding bath for forty minutes. Some of Oakley's relatives suggested that she may have been coloring her hair for some time. Perhaps the accident gave her a good reason to stop disguising the truth.[2]

Whatever the reason for the white hair, it seemed to mark the time of Oakley's decision to quit the Wild West. Oakley never returned to the Wild West after her accident in October 1901. Butler, now the breadwinner of the family, accepted a job with the Union Metallic Cartridge Company of Bridgeport, Connecticut. Oakley, wearing a curly brown wig, gave exhibitions and shot in matches.

Oakley's western image had become so well established that a play called *The Western Girl* was written for her. The press was kind to aging Annie Oakley and printed good reviews of the melodrama that opened in November 1902 and closed in March 1903.

Another False Report

Oakley spent a leisurely summer visiting relatives and friends in Ohio. She was considering a new play when a shocking newspaper story was released. "ANNIE OAKLEY ASKS COURT FOR MERCY—Famous Woman Crack Shot . . . Steals to Secure Cocaine" screamed the headline in a Chicago newspaper.[3]

The story was picked up by newspapers all over the country. Some ran the *Rochester Times* article, "ANNIE OAKLEY Famous Rifle Shot IS

The Western Girl, *a play written especially for Annie Oakley, received good reviews, but it closed after one season.*

DESTITUTE," word for word. Ernest Stout, the reporter who filed the original story, swore that a police investigator had verified that the arrested woman was the real Annie Oakley. After investigation, it was found that the impostor was Maude Fontenella, an actress who once had performed in a spoof on the Wild West show as "Any Oakley."[4]

Many newspapers retracted the story immediately and apologized in letters and editorials to Oakley. She would not be appeased. Over a period of five years, she sued fifty-five newspapers for damaging her reputation. Some of the lawsuits were settled out of court rather than through a jury trial. Other newspapers insisted on jury trials, where the jurors voted in Oakley's favor. There are no records of the total amount of money Oakley received from the lawsuits.

At the trials, Oakley was as sharp-tongued as the lawyers. When one lawyer asked for her definition of an education, she replied, "My idea of an education, is that it is a good thing when backed by common sense, and a very bad thing in the head of a cheap lawyer."[5]

When most of the lawsuits were behind her, Oakley joined Butler and proved time and again her proficiency with a gun. On August 18, 1908, she shot 483 targets out of 500 without taking a break. Her celebration was short-lived, however. Only fifteen minutes after she finished shooting, she received the news that her mother had died.[6]

Young Buffalo's Wild West

After ten years out of the spotlight, Oakley and Butler joined Young Buffalo's Wild West (not associated with Buffalo Bill's Wild West) in 1911. Butler resigned from the Union Metallic Cartridge Company to become Oakley's manager again. The press had either forgiven or forgotten Oakley's lawsuits because once again she received favorable reviews.

Fifty years old and somewhat plumper, Annie Oakley was well paid, but she no longer had top billing. She shared the spotlight with Curtis Liston, Captain O. G. Stevens, and seventy-eight-year-old Captain Adam Bogardus. Still, she received the ultimate praise when the show went to her hometown. The Greenville *Courier* urged every Darke County resident to attend Young Buffalo's Wild West to display love for Oakley, one of "Our Own."[7] She gave free tickets to the residents of Darke County Children's Home. After the show, she served the children free ice cream and other refreshments.

Annie Oakley rode in her last street parade and gave her last performance as a Wild West star on

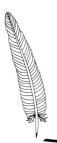

A Legend About "Annie Oakleys"

A newspaper from the early 1920s published the following article that explains what "Annie Oakleys" are:

Ban Johnson First Called Free Pass an "Annie Oakley"

One time in New York Ban Johnson was standing at the pass gate when a man presented a "non-transferable" ticket. Every time it was used the ticket taker punched a hole in it. There were so many holes in this one Ban Johnson remarked: "Well, that looks more like a target than a baseball pass." Now all free tickets are "Annie Oakleys."[8]

In 1911, when Annie Oakley joined Young Buffalo's Wild West, the show went to Greenville, Ohio. The whole town turned out to cheer Annie Oakley, their own star.

October 4, 1913. The Butlers had bought five acres and built a house on Hambrooks Bay near Cambridge, Maryland. Once their new house was ready, they planned to retire permanently.

Retirement and Dave

The Butlers settled in for their second retirement in another house built to Oakley's specifications. The walls of the living room were lined with shelves for Oakley's trophies and medals, and racks for her guns. Their bedroom window overlooked the bay, where Oakley could shoot ducks for their dinner.[9] The surrounding area was hunting country, where they could go through the woods looking for game.

Oakley had wanted a bird dog for a long time, and their new home was the ideal place for one. Butler went to East Market, Maryland, and found a black, white, and tan English setter in a kennel. He brought the dog home, and the Butlers named it Dave. Oakley began training Dave at once. He joined the Butlers in exhibitions where Oakley often shot an apple off his head. Dave was like a child to the Butlers and went everywhere with them.

Oakley had traveled too many years to settle in one place. She never really retired from shooting. "I couldn't do it," she said. "I went all to pieces under the care of a home. As Mr. Butler puts it, I am a complete failure as a housekeeper."[10]

In 1915, the Butlers joined the staff of the Carolina Hotel in Pinehurst, North Carolina. Butler was in charge of the skeet range. Oakley instructed women in the use of firearms and gave exhibitions of her shooting skills. She charged no fee for her lessons. She would be repaid, she said, if women became "shooting enthusiasts."[11] For seven years, the Butlers spent the winters in Pinehurst and the summers in New Hampshire, giving shooting lessons and exhibitions. Oakley proved again and again that she could do the same tricks with the same speed and accuracy that she had done in the Wild West arena.

Good-bye to an Old Friend

It was during those happy, carefree years that the Butlers' old friend, William F. "Buffalo Bill" Cody, died on January 20, 1917. Oakley wrote: "Goodbye old friend. The Sun setting over the mountain will pay its tribute to the resting place of the last of the great builders of the West, all of which you loved, and part of which you were."[12]

Just weeks after Cody's death, the United States entered World War I. Oakley offered to raise a women's regiment for home defense. Both the secretary of war and the president declined her offer. In 1917, women were expected to stay home while men went to war to protect their families and country. Determined to do her part, Oakley spent months traveling at her own expense from one army camp to another, doing exhibitions. "I am the happiest woman in the world because I had the opportunity to 'do my bit' in a way which was best suited to me," she told reporters.[13]

Oakley continued to do charity exhibitions. She became very active in the fight against tuberculosis. The lung disease had claimed two of her sisters and hundreds of American veterans of World War I. She not only donated money, but also had her gold medals melted and sold, and contributed the money to the tuberculosis sanitarium near Pinehurst.

In October 1922, Oakley appeared at the Brockton Fair in Massachusetts for her first paid performance in years. There were rumors that she was considering a comeback in show business. Yet an accident on November 9 ended any plans that she may have had.

Oakley and Butler were traveling with friends in a chauffeur-driven Cadillac near Daytona, Florida. The chauffeur lost control of the car, which jumped over an embankment and turned upside down. Oakley was pinned under the car. Her hip and right ankle were fractured. After six weeks in the hospital, Oakley moved to the Lakeview Hotel in Leesburg, Florida, where the Butlers often stayed. She had a brace on her leg and walked with crutches.

Another tragedy struck in February 1923, when Dave, the Butlers' faithful dog, was run over by a car and killed. They buried Dave under a tree in Leesburg and marked his grave with a simple stone. Letters of sympathy came from friends who knew how much Dave meant to them.[14]

Return to Darke County

When Oakley could travel, the Butlers visited her niece just a few miles from where Oakley was born. From there, they went to High Point, North Carolina, to attend the John Robinson Circus. In November, they stopped by the Pinehurst Fair.

After Annie Oakley retired from performing, she taught women how to shoot and held charity exhibitions.

After a few weeks in Pinehurst, visiting old friends, Oakley wanted to go home.

In December 1924, the Butlers left North Carolina for good and returned to Ohio. They took up residence in Dayton, near Oakley's sister Emily. For a year, Oakley kept up the pretense of good health. In reality, she was developing anemia, a lack of iron, which made her tired and pale.

Oakley realized she was slowly dying. She and Butler went to the Essex County Surrogate Court on October 25, 1925, where she made her final will. All of her money—a total of thirty-five thousand dollars—was divided among her relatives, with a greater portion going to her nieces than to her nephews. Her clothes and jewelry were to be divided among her three sisters.[15]

Butler filed his will the same day. In all the years the Butlers had been married, there was never a mention of his family. Yet he must have kept up with them because he left a thousand dollars each to his former wife, Elizabeth, and his daughter, Katie, who lived in Philadelphia. To his brother, John, he bequeathed all his guns and jewelry.[16]

In the late winter of 1925, Annie Oakley began writing her autobiography, but became too ill to finish it. By the spring of 1926, Oakley was spending about half her time in bed. Butler was also ill. In April, Will Rogers, a famous humorist and writer, came to visit the ailing couple. He was traveling the country, lecturing, and writing a weekly column. On April 30, his column paid tribute to Annie Oakley. He asked his readers to write to her. Over a thousand get-well letters from friends and strangers, however, could not improve Oakley's health. That

summer, she moved home to Darke County, where her niece Bonnie Blakeley could care for her.

Oakley insisted that Butler go to Pinehurst

Annie Oakley won the respect of people all over the world. Here, she wears a necklace given to her by Ludwig II, king of Bavaria, whom she saved from a bucking horse.

for the winter. He stopped in Detroit to meet Annie Fern Swartwout, who was supposed to escort him. He was too ill to go on. Oakley's niece prepared a room for him at her house.

In early October, Oakley asked Bonnie Blakeley to move her to a home in Greenville so she would be near the doctor. There, she made some changes in her will because Butler was so ill. She also made arrangements for her funeral.

On November 3, 1926, Annie Oakley slipped quietly away. Her family hid her death from the press at first so there could be a small funeral with only family and close friends. As she had instructed, her body was cremated and her ashes were placed in a silver loving cup given to her by the people of France in 1899.

Frank Butler, her husband of fifty years, died eighteen days later, on November 21. His body was returned to Darke County. On Thanksgiving Day, November 25, 1926, they were buried side by side in the old Brock Cemetery, she in her silver loving cup, and he in a coffin. Her simple headstone was inscribed:

> *Annie Oakley*
> *At Rest*
> *1926*

A LEGACY TO WOMEN

Annie Oakley was passionate about women's rights to make choices and to compete in certain areas of the male world. Oakley, as a sport shooter and hunter, bridged the world of women and men. She defied convention by competing with and becoming a champion shot among men.

Oakley's mother's example of strength and beliefs in basic Quaker principles were instilled in her daughter. Oakley believed in the essential worth of women. She was as competitive as any man. She demanded equal or higher pay for her skills. She had equality in her marriage.

Oakley was the model of an athletic woman who rode and shot in public. She challenged the prejudice in Wild West arenas against women performers. She campaigned for women shooters and opened the doors for cowgirls joining the circuits.

Oakley established a role model that was not threatening to either men or women. She proved that a woman could be skilled with a gun and a horse and still be feminine. Strength and skill did not mean coarse talk and masculine looks. She fulfilled people's expectations of womanhood while still excelling in a traditionally male-dominated job.[1] She set an example that women followed.

Oakley drew women audiences into the shooting exhibitions. Gradually, women and their daughters joined gun clubs and competed in matches. Because she was a respected hunter, women also began to hunt.

Women not only watched and tried to imitate Oakley, but also took lessons from her. She gave lessons in shooting, hunting, and camping. She began teaching in London and continued to give lessons until her accident in 1922.

An Argument for Women Shooters

Many people applauded Oakley's efforts to educate women about guns and the sport of using them. Others were critical, saying she encouraged women to neglect their "proper" duties. Oakley argued that hunting and shooting provided fine sport and exercise. Women could also use the skill to protect

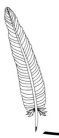

Women's Roles Change

By 1890, almost 4 million women (one out of seven) worked for wages outside their homes. Washington Territory gave women the right to vote in 1893 and Idaho followed in 1896. By 1900, the figure of employed women jumped to 5 million (one out of five).

themselves and their families from life-threatening attacks.[2]

In 1893, she issued a public statement about women shooters:

> I do not wish to be understood to mean by this that woman should sacrifice home and family duties entirely for outside pleasure . . . no opportunity should be lost by my sex of indulging in outdoor sports, pastimes, and recreations, which are at once healthy in their tone and results and womanly in their character.[3]

While Oakley broadened the limits of women's experiences, she still clung to her femininity. She enjoyed press reviews of her shooting skill, but she thrived on compliments about her ladylike behavior. She and Butler shaped an entertainment act that had universal appeal without compromising Oakley's Quaker background.

Small, demure Oakley sometimes surprised people with her toughness. She was not particularly ladylike when she called a Welshman "the ugliest monkey you ever saw."[4] She also showed her tough side when she challenged a lawyer by saying that education is "a very bad thing in the head of a cheap lawyer."[5]

In 1903, organizers of the Grand American Handicap announced that they would no longer use live birds in their annual event. The public had become very critical of the practice. However, Oakley continued to take part in live-bird shoots to prove herself against men. Live birds were the most difficult target of all. As long as men used them for targets, so would Oakley. She asked that the dead birds be sent to hospitals and orphanages to supplement their food.

When vaudeville became bawdy and the actresses began to wear too much makeup and dress scantily, Oakley's act reflected her own moral values. Butler, as her manager, booked his wife with shows that appealed to families.

Annie Oakley opened doors to new sports and activities for women all over the world.

Neither Oakley nor Butler smoked or drank alcohol, and they tried to separate themselves from people who did. In setting a good example, Oakley brought respectability to the entertainment field for women.

Oakley also proved that a woman could be married and have a successful career. The Butlers were fortunate that they seemed to be so well matched. Although Butler's performances were not as appealing to audiences as those of "Little Sure Shot," he played a critical role in the relationship. He promoted her career and gave her the spotlight. While she dedicated her life to being the best shot in the world, Butler dedicated himself to protecting Oakley from unpleasant problems. She lived most of her life in the public eye. Butler was always there in the shadows, working out contracts, publicity, travel arrangements, and equipment.

A Generous Woman

Oakley never took on the luxurious lifestyle of a "star." Although as they got older, both Oakley and Butler romanticized her early years, Oakley never forgot her roots. They lived comfortably but not lavishly. Oakley said, "If I ever spend one dollar foolishly I see tear-stained faces of little helpless children, beaten as I was."[6] The Butlers were generous with their money in helping Oakley's family. Her mother lived comfortably until her death because of the money that Oakley sent her every month. Oakley's nieces and nephews could expect packages throughout the year with school supplies and clothes and often a twenty-dollar bill as a special gift.

Oakley and Butler were also kind to poor children. They invited orphans to attend the Wild West as their guests. Oakley served free ice cream and other refreshments. They gave free exhibitions to raise money for children's hospitals and orphanages all over America and Europe.

American Indian children often played around the Butlers' tent and shared Oakley's lemonade and cookies. When other performers' children traveled with the shows, they, too, were included in Oakley's "tea parties."

Though she lacked a formal education herself, Oakley was well aware of the importance of education for women. Letters and thank-you notes indicate that she helped about twenty young women further their educations.[7]

World War I brought an end to the golden era of the Wild West shows that had made a legend of Annie Oakley. Increased traffic ended the big street parades. Americans began to flock to the new form of entertainment—motion pictures. Even before her death, the public remembered more about the legendary Annie Oakley than the real one.

Annie Oakley Legends Grow

Oakley had portrayed the model "Western Girl," but she had never been west of Ohio before becoming a performer. She had never shot bears nor battled American Indians. The public began confusing her dramatic roles and what was written about her with her real life. Her association with Sitting Bull was expanded and exploited by the press.

Oakley played the lead in three western dramas. In each, she rode, shot, and defeated evil in the American West. These roles added to the public's concept of Annie Oakley as a western girl.

A book about Oakley was published in England at the end of Oakley's London tour in 1889. Titled *The Rifle Queen*, it described a childhood of trapping wolves, fighting off train robbers, and other impossible escapades in Kansas, not Ohio. The only thing accurate in the dime novel with Annie Oakley as the heroine was her name. Still, many readers and journalists took the legends as truth and repeated the stories as fact.

Annie Oakley's name is as well known today as it was during her days with Buffalo Bill's Wild West. But the comic books, motion pictures, and television shows that have given her modern-day fame only vaguely resemble her life.

The legend that Oakley got her man, Frank Butler, by missing a shot and letting him win the contest

White-haired and older, Annie Oakley continued to ride her horse Highball and perform the skills that made her famous.

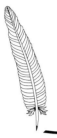

Women Shooters Increase

By the 1920s, several sports publications reported an increase in women shooters. One report titled "'Annie Oakleys' Increasing—Females Are Now Quite Generally Toting 'Shootin' Irons' Along With Their Precious Powder Puff and Lip Stick," advised gun merchants to "stock pistols for the ladies."[8]

began with a Barbara Stanwyck movie in 1935. When Herbert and Dorothy Fields, a brother-sister team, wrote a version of Oakley's life in the 1940s, the story was repeated. The Fieldses' manuscript was set to music by Irving Berlin and produced by Richard Rogers and Oscar Hammerstein. Ethel Merman starred in the musical, *Annie Get Your Gun*, on May 16, 1946, at the Imperial Theatre in New York City. The play ran for three years on Broadway with 1,159 performances.

The following years brought many adaptations of Oakley's life for movies, stage, and television. Mary Martin opened *Annie Get Your Gun* at the Texas State Fair in 1947. The national touring company performed the play in forty-nine cities. In 1950, Betty Hutton appeared in another film version of *Annie Get Your Gun*. It was billed as "The Biggest Musical Under the Sun in Technicolor." The film grossed over $4.5 million.[9] Mary Martin again starred as

Annie Oakley in a live television performance on November 27, 1957. Because of the poor quality of videotapes at that time, there is no record of the performance.

CBS premiered a series called *Annie Oakley and Tagg* in 1954. It attracted both boys and girls. In the eighty-one television episodes, Oakley was portrayed as a young woman who shot, rode, and often outwitted men. The series inspired fictionalized accounts of Oakley's life to be published for young readers. Although her legend has been immortalized through movies, books, and television shows, her real life was influential as well.

Annie Oakley was competitive and resolute. She lived by her values and beliefs in a rapidly changing world. She encouraged women to be independent thinkers and to take stands on important issues. She was a role model in opening doors to women where they had always been excluded. She showed women how to be strong without losing their femininity or dignity.

Annie Oakley's legend was a gift to show business. Her life was a gift to the women of the world.

CHRONOLOGY

1860—Born in Darke County, Ohio, on August 13.

1866—Jacob Moses (Oakley's father) died on February 11.

1870—Sent to live with Samuel and Nancy Ann Edington at Darke County Infirmary.

1870
–1872—Worked for the "wolf" family.

1874—Became a market hunter to provide money for her family.

1875—Won a shooting contest against Frank Butler on Thanksgiving Day.

1876—Married Frank Butler on August 23.

1882—Joined Butler in a trick-shooting performance on May 1 and took the stage name Annie Oakley.

1884—Met Sitting Bull and was adopted as his daughter; Joined Sells Brothers Circus and was billed as a markswoman for the first time.

1885—Joined Buffalo Bill's Wild West in April and Butler became her manager.

1887—Went to England with the Wild West in April for Queen Victoria's Golden Jubilee; Performed for Queen Victoria on May 12; Left the Wild West and returned with Butler to New York in the winter.

1888—Joined Pawnee Bill's Wild West; Set the American record for shooting doubles; Appeared in her first dramatic role in *Deadwood Dick, or the Sunbeam of the Sierras*, on December 22.

1889—Reunited with Buffalo Bill's Wild West.

1894—Starred in a Thomas Edison film.

1901—Injured in a train accident on October 28, which ended her career with Buffalo Bill's Wild West.

1903
–1908—Sued fifty-five newspapers for printing a false story about her being a drug addict.

1913—Gave her last performance as a Wild West star on October 4.

1922—Injured in a car accident on November 9.

1926—Died on November 3 in Greenville, Ohio, near her birthplace.

CHAPTER NOTES

Chapter 1

1. Annie Oakley, *The Story of My Life* (n.p., 1926), chap. 4, n.p.
2. Ibid.
3. Annie Oakley, "Notes on Shooting," *Shooting and Fishing*, n.d., Annie Oakley Scrapbook, n.p.
4. Walter Havighurst, *Annie Oakley of the Wild West* (New York: The Macmillan Company, 1954), p. 14.
5. Ibid.
6. Ibid., p. 15.
7. Ibid.
8. Isabelle S. Sayers, *Annie Oakley and Buffalo Bill's Wild West* (New York: Dover Publications, Inc., 1981), p. 5.
9. Oakley, chap. 4, n.p.
10. Shirl Kasper, *Annie Oakley* (Norman: University of Oklahoma Press, 1992), p. 15.
11. Glenda Riley, *The Life and Legacy of Annie Oakley* (Norman: University of Oklahoma Press, 1994), p. 16.
12. Kasper, p. 16.
13. Clifford Lindsey Alderman, *Annie Oakley and the World of Her Time* (New York: Macmillan, 1979), p. 17.
14. Oakley, chap. 4, n.p.
15. Ibid.
16. Alderman, p. 17.

Chapter 2

1. Annie Fern Swartwout, *Annie Oakley Her Life and Times*, 2nd ed., ed. Ronald Swartwout (New York: Carlton Press, Inc., 1970), p. 11.
2. Annie Oakley, *The Story of My Life* (n.p., 1926), chap. 1, n.p.
3. Ibid.
4. Ibid.
5. Shirl Kasper, *Annie Oakley* (Norman: University of Oklahoma Press, 1992), p. 5.
6. Oakley, chap. 1, n.p.
7. Ibid.
8. Ibid.
9. Ibid., chap. 2, n.p.

10. Ibid.

11. Ibid.

12. Ibid.

13. Ibid.

14. Glenda Riley, *The Life and Legacy of Annie Oakley* (Norman: University of Oklahoma Press, 1994), p. 8.

Chapter 3

1. Annie Oakley, *The Story of My Life* (n.p., 1926), chap. 2, n.p.

2. Ibid., chap. 4, n.p.

3. Annie Oakley, *Powders I Have Used* (Wilmington, Del.: Dupont Powder Company, 1914), p. 1. Courtesy of Dorchester County Public Library, Cambridge, Md.

4. Shirl Kasper, *Annie Oakley* (Norman: University of Oklahoma Press, 1992), p. 7.

5. Unidentified clipping, n.d., Annie Oakley Scrapbook, 1912–on, n.p. Microfilm, Courtesy of Buffalo Bill Historical Center, Cody, Wyo.

6. Glenda Riley, *The Life and Legacy of Annie Oakley* (Norman: University of Oklahoma Press, 1994), p. 12.

7. "Women Should Be Able to Shoot," *The Times*, n.d., Annie Oakley Scrapbook, 1902–1908, n.p.

8. Oakley, *The Story of My Life*, chap. 4, n.p.

9. Walter Havighurst, *Annie Oakley of the Wild West* (New York: The Macmillan Company, 1954), p. 12.

10. Cliford Lindsey Alderman, *Annie Oakley and the World of Her Time* (New York: Macmillan, 1979), p. 14.

11. Oakley, *The Story of My Life*, chap. 4, n.p.

12. Havighurst, p. 18.

13. Riley, p. 17.

14. Oakley, *The Story of My Life*, chap. 5, n.p.

Chapter 4

1. Annie Fern Swartwout, *Annie Oakley Her Life and Times*, 2nd ed., ed. Ronald Swartwout (New York: Carlton Press, Inc., 1970), p. 42.

2. Annie Oakley, *The Story of My Life* (n.p., 1926), chap. 5, n.p.

3. Glenda Riley, *The Life and Legacy of Annie Oakley* (Norman: University of Oklahoma Press, 1994), p. 21.

4. Walter Havighurst, *Annie Oakley of the Wild West* (New York: The Macmillan Company, 1954), p. 69.

5. Ibid., p. 24.

6. Riley, p. 21.

7. Isabelle S. Sayers, *Annie Oakley and Buffalo Bill's Wild West* (New York: Dover Publications, Inc., 1981), p. 9.

8. Annie Oakley, "Notes on Shooting," *Shooting and Fishing,* n.d., Annie Oakley Scrapbook, n.p.

9. Riley, p. 145.

10. Ibid., p. 27.

11. Ibid., pp. 25–26.

12. Shirl Kasper, *Annie Oakley* (Norman: University of Oklahoma Press, 1992), p. 32.

13. Oakley, *The Story of My Life,* chap. 6, n.p.

14. Ellen Levine, *Ready, Aim, Fire! The Real Adventures of Annie Oakley* (New York: Scholastic, Inc., 1989), p. 54.

15. Oakley, chap. 6, n.p.

16. Don Russell, *The Lives and Legends of Buffalo Bill* (Norman: University of Oklahoma Press, 1960), p. 35.

Chapter 5

1. Don Russell, *The Lives and Legends of Buffalo Bill* (Norman: University of Oklahoma Press, 1960), p. 90.

2. Ibid., p. 89.

3. Ibid., p. 159.

4. Ibid., p. 176.

5. Ibid., p. 290.

6. Ibid., p. 295.

7. Annie Oakley, *The Story of My Life* (n.p., 1926), chap. 6, n.p.

8. Ibid.

9. Russell, p. 35.

10. Oakley, chap. 6, n.p.

11. Ibid.

12. Isabelle S. Sayers, *Annie Oakley and Buffalo Bill's Wild West* (New York: Dover Publications, Inc., 1981), p. 22.

13. Glenda Riley, *The Life and Legacy of Annie Oakley* (Norman: University of Oklahoma Press, 1994), p. 149.

14. Oakley, chap. 7, n.p.

Chapter 6

1. Annie Oakley, *The Story of My Life* (n.p., 1926), chap. 7, n.p.

2. Ibid.

3. Glenda Riley, *The Life and Legacy of Annie Oakley* (Norman: University of Oklahoma Press, 1994), p. 34.

4. Shirl Kasper, *Annie Oakley* (Norman: University of Oklahoma Press, 1992), p. 61.

5. Ibid., p. 62.

6. Oakley, chap. 7, n.p.

7. Oakley, chap. 8, n.p.

8. "A Darke County Girl," *The Courier*, Saturday, May 3, 1913, Annie Oakley Scrapbook, n.p.

9. Clifford Lindsey Alderman, *Annie Oakley and the World of Her Time* (New York: Macmillan, 1979), p. 44.

10. Ibid.

11. Oakley, chap. 8, n.p.

12. *The New York Herald*, November 25, 1886, Annie Oakley Scrapbook, 1887–1891, n.p.

13. New York *Clipper*, March 4, 1887, Annie Oakley Scrapbook, 1887–1891, n.p.

14. Newark (N.J.) *Sunday Call*, n.d., Annie Oakley Scrapbook, 1887–1891, n.p.

15. Kasper, p. 64.

16. Unidentified clipping, n.d., Annie Oakley Scrapbook, 1887–1891, n.p.

17. Ibid.

18. Ibid.

19. Oakley, chap. 8, n.p.

Chapter 7

1. London *Times*, April 15, 1887, Annie Oakley Scrapbook, 1887–1891, n.p.

2. Annie Oakley, *The Story of My Life* (n.p., 1926), chap. 9, n.p.

3. Shirl Kasper, "Annie Oakley: The Magical Year in London," *Montana The Magazine of Western History*, vol. 42, no. 2, Spring 1992, p. 27.

4. *Shooting*, 128 Strand, London, December 14, 1887, Annie Oakley Scrapbook, 1887–1891, n.p.

5. Oakley, chap. 9, n.p.

6. Clifford Lindsey Alderman, *Annie Oakley and the World of Her Time* (New York: Macmillan, 1979), p. 53.

7. Oakley, chap. 9, n.p.

8. Ibid.

9. *Shooting and Fishing*, n.d., Annie Oakley Scrapbook, 1887–1891, n.p.

10. Glenda Riley, *The Life and Legacy of Annie Oakley* (Norman: University of Oklahoma, 1992), p. 88.

11. "Miss Oakley's Pigeon Shooting," n.d., Annie Oakley Scrapbook, 1887–1891, n.p.

12. Annie Fern Swartwout, *Annie Oakley Her Life and Times*, 2nd ed., ed. Ronald Swartwout (New York: Carlton Press, Inc., 1970), p. 102.

13. Oakley, chap. 10, n.p.

14. Ibid.

15. Ibid.

16. Swartwout, p. 102.

17. Oakley, chap. 10, n.p.

18. Ibid.

19. Ibid.

20. *The World*, January 8, 1888, Annie Oakley Scrapbook, 1887–1891, n.p.

Chapter 8

1. New York *Clipper*, May 5, 1888, Annie Oakley Scrapbook, 1887–1891, n.p.

2. Annie Oakley, *The Story of My Life* (n.p., 1926), chap. 11, n.p.

3. Ibid.

4. Shirl Kasper, *Annie Oakley* (Norman: University of Oklahoma Press, 1992), p. 97.

5. Unidentified clipping, n.d., Annie Oakley Scrapbook, 1887–1891, n.p.

6. Annie Fern Swartwout, *Annie Oakley Her Life and Times*, 2nd ed., ed. Ronald Swartwout (New York: Carlton Press, Inc., 1970), p. 109.

7. "BEATEN BY A GIRL Miss Oakley Outshoots Fred Knoll— She was Modest About It," Baltimore *American and Commercial Advertiser*, Wednesday, October 31, 1888, Annie Oakley Scrapbook, 1887–1891, n.p.

8. "Miss Oakley Breaks Record," Philadelphia, *The Item*, December 19, 1888, n.p.

9. Kasper, p. 95.

10. Ibid.

11. Isabelle S. Sayers, *Annie Oakley and Buffalo Bill's Wild West* (New York: Dover Publications, Inc., 1981), p. 41.

12. Paterson *Daily Guardian*, n.d., Annie Oakley Scrapbook, 1887–1891, n.p.

13. Oakley, chap. 12, n.p.

14. Ibid.

15. Unidentified clipping, n.d., Annie Oakley Scrapbook, 1921–1925, n.p.

16. Oakley, chap. 12, n.p.

17. Ibid.

18. Ibid.

Chapter 9

1. Annie Oakley, *The Story of My Life* (n.p., 1926), chap. 13, n.p.

2. Unidentified clipping, n.d., Annie Oakley Scrapbook, 1887–1891, n.p.

3. Oakley, chap. 15, n.p.

4. Shirl Kasper, *Annie Oakley* (Norman: University of Oklahoma Press, 1992), p. 117.

5. New York *Press*, August 11, 1894, Annie Oakley Scrapbook, 1893–1895, n.p.

6. Annie Fern Swartwout, *Annie Oakley Her Life and Times*, 2nd ed., ed. Ronald Swartwout (New York: Carlton Press, Inc., 1970), p. 138.

7. Isabelle S. Sayers, *Annie Oakley and Buffalo Bill's Wild West* (New York: Dover Publications, Inc., 1981), p. 54.

8. Hereford *Times*, December 28, 1894, Annie Oakley Scrapbook, 1893–1895, n.p.

9. Knoxville *Sentinel*, May 1, 1899, Annie Oakley Scrapbook, 1896–1901, n.p.

10. Kasper, p. 166.

11. Swartwout, p. 175.

Chapter 10

1. *American Field*, n.d., Annie Oakley Scrapbook, 1892–1898, n.p.

2. Glenda Riley, *The Life and Legacy of Annie Oakley* (Norman: University of Oklahoma Press, 1994), p. 61.

3. Chicago *Examiner and American*, August 11, 1903, Annie Oakley Scrapbook, 1902–1908, n.p.

4. Isabelle S. Sayers, *Annie Oakley and Buffalo Bill's Wild West* (New York: Dover Publications, Inc., 1981), p. 79.

5. Unidentified clipping, n.d., Annie Oakley Scrapbook, 1903–1905, n.p.

6. *American Field*, Annie Oakley Scrapbook, n.d., n.p.

7. Greenville (Ohio) *Courier*, May 3, 1913, Annie Oakley Scrapbook, 1912–on, n.p.

8. Unidentified clipping, n.d., Annie Oakley Scrapbook, 1921–1925, n.p.

9. Helen Chappel, "Sure as Shootin'," Baltimore *Sun Magazine*, October 1, 1995, n.p. Courtesy of Dorchester County Public Library, Cambridge, Md.

10. Philadelphia *Public Ledger*, May 18, 1919, Annie Oakley Scrapbook, 1912–on, n.p.

11. Shirl Kasper, *Annie Oakley* (Norman: University of Oklahoma Press, 1992), p. 207.

12. Pinehurst (N.C.) *Outlook*, January 20, 1917, Annie Oakley Scrapbook, 1912–on, n.p.

13. Ibid.; *New American Shooter*, October 1918, Annie Oakley Scrapbook, 1912–on, n.p.

14. Kasper, p. 230.

15. Ibid., p. 236.

16. Ibid., p. 239.

Chapter 11

1. Glenda Riley, "Annie Oakley Creating the Cowgirl," *Montana The Magazine of Western History*, vol. 45, no. 3, Summer 1995, p. 33.

2. Annie Oakley, "Ladies Should Use Firearms," *Shooting and Hunting*, n.d., Annie Oakley Scrapbook, 1887–1891, n.p.

3. London *Shooting Times*, August 26, 1893, Annie Oakley Scrapbook, 1893–1895, n.p.

4. Shirl Kasper, *Annie Oakley* (Norman: University of Oklahoma Press, 1992), p. 76.

5. Unidentified clipping, n.d., Annie Oakley Scrapbook, 1903–1905, n.p.

6. Annie Oakley, *The Story of My Life* (n.p., 1926), chap. 3, n.p.

7. Glenda Riley, *The Life and Legacy of Annie Oakley* (Norman: University of Oklahoma Press, 1994), p. 128.

8. "'Annie Oakleys' Increasing—Females Are Now Quite Generally Toting 'Shootin' Irons' Along With Their Precious Powder Puff and Lip Stick," *The Sporting Goods Dealer*, n.d., Annie Oakley Scrapbook, 1921–1925, n. p.

9. Isabelle S. Sayers, *Annie Oakley and Buffalo Bill's Wild West* (New York: Dover Publications, Inc., 1981), p. 87.

GLOSSARY

anemia—A condition in which the blood is deficient in red blood cells, usually caused by a lack of iron.

benefactor—One that makes a gift or bequest.

blood poisoning—A toxic condition resulting from the spread of bacteria from an infection.

boisterous—Expression of exuberance and high spirits.

bore—A cylindrical hollow tube or gun barrel.

buckboard—A four-wheel vehicle with a floor made of long springy boards.

destitute—Suffering extreme poverty.

drop—The fit of the stock (wooden part) of a gun on a shooter's shoulder for best advantage in aiming at a target.

exhibition—A public showing (as of works of art, subjects of manufacture).

game—Wild animals hunted for sport or food.

gauge—The size of a shotgun barrel's inner diameter.

gingham—A cotton fabric, usually striped or checked.

homespun—Spun or made at home.

leech—A bloodsucking worm.

mortgage—Payment owed to a moneylender for property or a home.

negotiation—Action or process of conferring with another so as to arrive at the settlement of some matter.

opponent—One who takes an opposite position.

regiment—A military unit of soldiers.

romanticize—To treat as idealized or heroic.

sanitarium—An establishment that provides therapy combined with a regimen (as of diet and exercise) for treatment or rehabilitation.

sharpshooter—A good marksman; a person skilled in shooting at a mark or target.

spectator—One who looks on or watches.

stock—The wooden part of a gun that fits against the shoulder.

target—A small round shield; a mark to shoot at.

tavern—An inn.

transaction—An exchange or sale of goods, services, or funds.

tuberculosis—A highly contagious disease that primarily affects the lungs.

FURTHER READING

Collier, Edmund. *The Story of Annie Oakley*. New York: Grosset & Dunlap, 1956.

Graves, Charles P. *Annie Oakley: The Shooting Star*. New York: Chelsea Juniors, A division of Chelsea House Publishers, 1991.

Kirk, Rhina. *Circus Heroes and Heroines*. Maplewood, N.J.: Hammond, Inc., 1972.

Kraske, Robert. *Daredevils Do Amazing Things*. New York: Random House, 1978.

Newton, David E. *Hunting*. New York: Franklin Watts, 1992.

Patent, Dorothy Henshaw. *A Family Goes Hunting*. New York: Clarion Books, 1991.

Quackenbush, Robert. *Who's That Girl With the Gun? A Story of Annie Oakley*. New York: Prentice Hall Books for Young Readers, 1988.

Spies, Karen Bornemann. *Buffalo Bill Cody: Western Legend*. Springfield, N.J.: Enslow Publishers, Inc., 1998.

Spinner, Stephanie. *Little Sure Shot: The Story of Annie Oakley*. New York: Random House, 1993.

Stevenson, Augusta. *Buffalo Bill: Frontier Daredevil*. New York: Macmillan Child Group, 1991.

Wilson, Ellen. *Annie Oakley*. New York: Macmillan Child Group, 1989.

INDEX